THE COMING RESURRECTION OF THE DEAD

THE COMING RESURRECTION OF THE DEAD

Now if Christ be preached
that he rose from the dead,
how say some among you that
there is no resurrection of the dead?
I Corinthians 15:12

JOHN METCALFE

THE PUBLISHING TRUST
Church road, Tylers Green, Penn, Buckinghamshire

Printed and Published by the
John Metcalfe Publishing Trust
Church Road, Tylers Green
Penn, Buckinghamshire

–

Distributed by Trust Representatives
and Agents world-wide

In the Far East

Bethany, Orchard Point P.O. Box 0373
Singapore 912313

–

–

First Published 2001

–

ISBN 1 870039 85 8

–

**This work is available at less than the
cost of production through subsidies on
the part of the John Metcalfe Publishing
Trust. The Author waives all royalties in
favour of the Trust, a Registered Charity.**

CONTENTS

THE COMING RESURRECTION OF THE DEAD

IN opening the truth of the coming resurrection of the dead, I Corinthians 15:1-58, the apostle Paul commences by declaring to the *ecclesia* at Corinth the evangel which he preached unto them, which they received, and in which they stood.

But why declare this? Because of the error of some among them, who, not only forgetting what they had received, substituted that which struck at the heart of the evangel.

What struck at the heart of the evangel? The denial of the resurrection of Christ from the dead.

The apostle shows that without belief in the resurrection, they had neither the evangel, nor the faith, nor yet any hope whatever either in this life or the next. Hence his insistence upon the truth that the resurrection of Christ lay at the very heart of the apostles' witness and doctrine in the belief of which alone salvation was assured.

'Moreover, brethren, I declare unto you the gospel which I preached unto you, which also ye have received, and wherein ye stand; by which ye are saved, if ye keep in memory what I preached unto you, unless ye have believed in vain', I Corinthians 15:1,2.

As was the case with each successive instance following on from the *first* occasion on which the apostle specifically addressed the *ecclesia* at Corinth *as assembled together*–'For *first* of *all*, when ye come together in the *ecclesia*', I Corinthians 11:18– so in this the *last* instance: *the passage is corrective.*

Throughout this long chapter–I Corinthians 15:1-58–the apostle is occupied with the correction of their error regarding the resurrection of the dead.

This is revealed in the following crucial statement, put in the form of a question, concerning the departure from the truth of certain at Corinth: 'Now if Christ be preached'–by all the apostolic eyewitnesses testifying together with one voice–'that he rose from the dead, *how say some among you that there is no resurrection of the dead?*', I Corinthians 15:12.

The challenge sounded out by Paul's question in this place provides the reason for the answering corrective doctrine which he declares everywhere else, from the first verse to the last.

The fact that the apostle reiterates the truth of the evangel 'by which ye are saved'; that this must be 'kept in memory'; and that faith must be kept alive–'unless ye have believed in vain'–go together to demonstrate that vague statements, recited creeds, sentimental feelings, simple professions of an otherwise undefined 'Jesus', much less a mere 'acceptance' or 'committal', *are not enough* – according to I Corinthians chapter 15 – to warrant either the apostolic meaning of believing, or that of the faith of the evangel, or, of course, of salvation itself.

How does I Corinthians 15 demonstrate this?

Because it *insists* on the truth of the resurrection being integral to the evangel; that it is the evangel *itself* that saves; and that faith cannot respect Christ, nor can Christ be believed upon, *save through that evangel given by the Father, spoken by the Son, witnessed by the Holy Ghost, and declared by the apostles.*

And *that* evangel incorporates the resurrection.

So, 'how say some among you that there is no resurrection of the dead?', I Corinthians 15:12.

The faith that saves, the evangel that is to be believed, the apostles' doctrine that declares the word of life, the doctrine of Christ that brings into union with the Father and the Son, in a word, *this* evangel declared by Paul, I Corinthians 15:1, finds its strength in the sum of its parts. '*It* is the power of God unto salvation', Romans 1:16.

All, but *all*, the parts are essential rightly and in balance to declare him who *is* the truth.

To believe in Christ is to believe *the evangel* of Christ. To profess a 'Jesus' or a 'Christ' *without* that evangel is to be *anti* Christ. To profess only a part of the evangel, discarding another part – such as the resurrection – evinces a false profession: no true faith at all.

Christ is expressed, and expresses himself, through the evangel, the whole of the evangel, and nothing other than the evangel. This was declared once for all by the eyewitnesses, the chosen apostles. It was 'declared' unto us.

3

The word of God came not out from us, it came unto us only. Then, we cannot discard what we will, retain what we wish, or invent what we want.

The sole expression of Christ is in the truths of the evangel, completely in order, perfectly in proportion, and wholly in balance: then and there the glorious evangel shines, and shines in the face of Jesus Christ.

It is *this* that is to be both preached and believed: *all of it; not just some of it; much less a 'Jesus' without it; or, worse, some alternative to it.*

Christ, who is the truth, is expressed in the truths of the evangel, *all of which together as a whole constitute the truth, from which any missing part* – such as the resurrection of Christ from the dead – *nullifies the whole.*

Observe that it is this verity by which the Spirit inspires the apostle in his corrective doctrine concerning the truth of the resurrection in I Corinthians chapter 15.

First; the apostolic declaration affirms the indispensability of the truth of the resurrection to the integrity of the evangel of Christ, I Corinthians 15:1-11.

If so, it behoved the apostle to clarify that evangel as a whole, as he declared it when first he preached to the Corinthians: 'Moreover, brethren, I declare unto you the gospel which I preached unto you,

'which also ye have received, and wherein ye stand; by which also ye are saved,

'if ye keep in memory what I preached unto you' – or, more literally '*by which also ye are being saved, if ye hold fast what word I evangelized to you*' – 'unless ye have believed in vain.

'For I delivered unto you first of all that which I also received.'

At this point the apostle forthwith but briefly summarizes for their benefit and memory that very evangel which he had evangelized to them 'first of all', or, *in the first place*, I Corinthians 15:1-3.

So that before commencing his brief summary – or definition – of the evangel in its essence, the apostle recalls to their remembrance the circumstances and manner of their having received it at the time, and, indeed, of their then holding it fast as a whole.

To this end the apostle states the things in which he himself was – or else had been – active. Firstly, why he was writing this at that present time: 'I declare unto you', present tense, verse 1. Thus he is about to recall to them in writing that which he had done for them in the past.

It was to be a written declaration stating the apostle's current recollection of his past activity – and their beginnings – at Corinth.

His past activity? That which he had done for them in the beginning? He had preached the gospel unto them. Here the apostle recalls the very first thing which he had done at Corinth: 'I declare' – now – 'unto you the gospel which *I preached*' – then – 'unto you', I Corinthians 15:1.

The first verb is in the present, the second in the past tense.

This is the apostle's recollection of what he had done for them at the very beginning when he came to Corinth.

'I declare unto you *the evangel which I evangelized to you*', verse 1. He repeats this in verse 2: 'I preached unto you', or, literally, '*what word I evangelized unto you.*'

He is going to bring home to them at present that which he had preached unto them–the evangel which he had evangelized–in the past.

Why? Because some among them said *now* what they had neither heard, nor would have dared to say *then*. What was this? That there is no resurrection of the dead, verse 12.

But *this*, declares Paul, *utterly contradicts the evangel by which they had been evangelized: it attempts to overturn that word which he had evangelized unto them when first he came among them.*

Then, he is going to jolt their memories by reiterating the evangel by which they should be saved: 'unless ye have believed in vain', verse 2.

In declaring again the evangel which he had evangelized long before, the apostle is emphasizing the fact–the *obvious* fact–that when first he came to Corinth, he had preached *the evangel*, and that in its very essence, verse 1.

If so, what they heard, received, and believed *then*, was 'the word of truth, the evangel of your salvation', Ephesians 1:13. Observe, it is *the* evangel.

There is none other: 'But though we, or an angel from heaven, preach any other evangel unto you than that which we have preached unto you, let him be accursed. As we said before, so say I now again, If any man preach any other evangel unto you than that ye have received, let him be accursed', Galatians 1:8,9.

Observe that the apostle is speaking of a *body of truth*, namely, the *body of truth which declares the person and work of Christ.* That body of truth was the sum of every single one of its essential parts, of which none was more significant than that which declared *the resurrection of Christ from the dead.*

6

Hence Paul's emphasis on the evangel strikes at the enormity of the presumption adopted by 'some among you' that either the evangel, or any part of the evangel, could ever be considered as optional, subject to mutation, or else alterable: 'How say some among you that there is no resurrection of the dead?', verse 12.

This evangel is described under various terms in the new testament: for example it *is* the new testament. It is called 'the doctrine of Christ.'

This doctrine declares the things – *things*, mark it – that constitute those essential, related, and balanced truths by which the Holy Ghost through the apostles enshrined the truth, the whole truth, and nothing but the truth concerning Jesus Christ, namely, the 'things most surely believed among us', Luke 1:1.

'But continue thou' – though all about seemed to be falling away – 'continue *thou* in the *things* which thou hast learned and hast been assured of, knowing of whom thou hast learned them', II Timothy 3:14.

What things? 'The form of sound words, which thou hast heard of me, in faith and love which is in Christ Jesus', II Timothy 1:13. This 'form' – delineation; pattern – answers to those truths which as a whole constitute the evangel of Christ.

This is the apostles' doctrine, in which the early *ecclesia* continued steadfastly, Acts 2:42. It is the word, in the truth of which, if they continued, then were they Christ's disciples indeed; 'and ye shall know the truth, and the truth shall make you free', John 8:31,32.

Again, the evangel is called 'the faith once delivered unto the saints', Jude 3. Delivered to the saints, note, not the academics.

Man's creation of a separate priestly caste – of 'clergy' ordained to administer 'sacraments' to the 'laity' – largely secured the apostasy, in which education took the place of revelation;

clerisy took the place of Spirit-filled saints; divinity faculties took the place of the calling, discipline and teaching of Jesus Christ through the Holy Ghost from heaven; and 'theology'– whatever *that* means – took the place of 'the faith once delivered unto the saints'.

Now, *that* faith is what the apostle calls *the evangel*, I Corinthians 15:1,2.

Whence take notice that the apostles were sent to evangelize, and what they evangelized was *the evangel*. The way in which this was received was by *believing*.

The ministers of Jesus Christ received grace and apostleship 'for obedience to the faith among all nations, for his name', Romans 1:5.

Those who heard and received such apostolic ministers sent 'into all the world to preach the gospel', Mark 16:15, 'obeyed from the heart that form of doctrine which was delivered to them', Romans 6:17, and, 'He that believeth and is baptized shall be saved; but he that believeth not shall be damned', Mark 16:16.

Where 'believing' means wholly submitting to and receiving from the heart *all the evangel*, in *all its parts*, and *in the whole*, that is, sincerely yielding the whole-hearted obedience of faith to the entirety of the apostles' doctrine, the doctrine of Christ, the form of sound words, the faith once delivered, the new testament, the word of truth, namely, *the evangel*.

If so, this is to come to *the knowledge* of the truth. For it is *knowledge* – in the inward and spiritual reception of it – to which one responds in the evangel. Hence those who believed were 'transformed by the renewing of their *mind*.' It is *the truth* that is believed.

Then, it is not just the *experience* of Christ: above all, it is the *knowledge* of Christ. The first is *felt*: the last is *believed*. Experience—true or false—only concerns that which one feels about him personally; but believing concerns *what he is in himself*.

One *feels* subjective experience, and this is within *oneself*; but one *believes* objective doctrine, and *that* is what *he* is, *in and of himself*.

In the one case everything is confined within *you*; but in the other instance everything is expanded to *him*. That is what is meant by believing.

One believes *the evangel*, and Paul declares that this is exactly the truth which he preached when he evangelized the evangel at the beginning in Corinth. If so, now, 'How say some among you that there is no resurrection of the dead?', verse 12.

Those 'some among you' would never have said that at the beginning. Then, what Paul preached unto them, they, together with all, heartily received. Had they forgotten? They must needs keep in memory the evangel which the apostle evangelized unto them, because *nothing else, and nothing less* would save them.

Do they contend? Then must the apostle conclude that they had believed in vain?

'I declare unto you the evangel which I evangelized unto you, which also ye have received, and wherein ye stand; by which also ye are saved, if ye keep in memory what I evangelized unto you, unless ye have believed in vain.

'For I delivered unto you first of all that which I also received', I Corinthians 15:1-3. In that Paul says that he *delivered* the evangel, it follows that nothing that he preached was initiated, contrived, or invented by him. It was not his opinion in religion: it was his part faithfully to deliver the message on behalf of the sender.

What he delivered was wholly the message of the one from whom he had received it: the apostle neither added to it, sub-tracted from it, multiplied it, divided it, or substituted anything of his own – or anyone else's – in place of it: what was given to him – no more, no less – that he delivered unto them.

It was not even that he delivered his own experience of Christ, that is to say, his *own* testimony. He received what he was to deliver, and that was what he passed on faithfully.

It was not what Christ had done to or in him: that would be *his* testimony: it was what God had done in Christ; that was *God's* testimony. The message was the evangel of God concerning his Son, a message complete within itself.

It was *God's* testimony concerning his own Son, which Paul had received of him by the Holy Ghost under the anointing. It was the *testimony of Christ* which he had received from God out of heaven in its entirety, and passed on to them, delivering that message to them faithfully, exactly as he had received it.

His place had been to act as a messenger on behalf of the one who had sent him, an ambassador, a post, who, having this charge, did no more than deliver the message that was his responsibility to pass on to the recipients.

This message – the evangel – Paul describes as 'that which I also *received*'. How did he receive it? He received it in a unique, apostolic manner. He received it from the Father, by the Son, through the Holy Ghost: 'I certify you, brethren, that the evangel which was preached of me is not after man. For I neither received it of man, neither was I taught it, but by the revelation of Jesus Christ', Galatians 1:11,12.

As to that, the Son himself – uniquely and apostolically – appeared to Paul, saying, 'I have appeared unto thee for this purpose, to make thee a minister and a witness both of these things which thou hast seen, and of those things in the which I will appear unto thee', Acts 26:16.

Hence Paul speaks of 'the dispensation of the grace of God which is given me to you-ward: how that by revelation he made known unto me the mystery', Ephesians 3:2,3.

And again, referring to the evangel, Paul says, 'Whereof I was made a minister, according to the gift of the grace of God given unto me by the effectual working of his power. Unto me, who am less than the least of all saints, is this grace given, that I should preach among the Gentiles the unsearchable riches of Christ', Ephesians 3:7,8.

Once more: 'I am made a minister, according to the dispensation of God which is given to me for you, to fulfil the word of God', Colossians 1:25.

Then, this evangel which the apostle delivered unto the *ecclesia* at Corinth was that which he had received by revelation from God, concerning the person and work of Christ, a dispensation having been given to him to deliver as he had received it, which was what he had done faithfully throughout his ministry, and not least at Corinth.

What he received was all of God, and what he delivered was all of God, and, moreover, he had done so as sent, delivering the evangel not in word only, but also in power, and in the Holy Ghost, and in much assurance, I Thessalonians 1:5.

Thus he declares unto them in this present epistle the things that he had done when first he came to them in times past: he had evangelized the evangel. He had delivered unto them the evangel. And, before ever he came to them, having been called to the apostolate, he had received that evangel by revelation from the Father, by the Son, and through the Holy Ghost.

Moreover, this same evangel was a profound mystery, it brought into the fellowship of the mystery: nevertheless, not all its profundity, but the clarity of its first principles, the evangel of Christ in its essence, 'first of all' Paul had delivered to the *ecclesia* at Corinth.

At this point in I Corinthians 15:3 Paul enunciates the essence of the evangel even as 'first of all' he had delivered unto them that which he had received of God.

He declares the things – mark that: the *things* – most surely believed among us, Luke 1:1, in which, beginning with the person of Christ, he proceeds to affirm his death, burial, and resurrection.

Next he enumerates in order the chosen eyewitnesses of these attested and verified *historical facts*, evidently seen by those who ate and drank with him after he rose from the dead, Acts 10:39-42.

'For I delivered unto you first of all that which I also received, how that Christ died for our sins according to the scriptures.' How much is revealed by this opening declaration of the evangel! That the Messiah, the Christ, promised ever since the foundation of the world, *had actually come*. Moreover, he had come *to die*. Further, he *had* actually died.

But his was no ordinary death. How could it be? What? Of the Messiah, who should come into the world, known – however dimly – of all nations even to the ends of the earth, as saith the wise men from the east, 'Where is he that is born king of the Jews?'.

Likewise the Samaritan woman: 'I know that Messias cometh, which is called Christ: when he is come, he will tell us all things', John 4:25.

And this dim flicker persevered in the consciousness of all nations – as 'To the unknown God', Acts 17:23 – however enlightened or debased; but now, saith Paul, *He has come*. And *come to die*.

Why? Because 'Christ Jesus came into the world to save sinners', I Timothy 1:15, and, if so, by dying in their place.

Whose place? Directly in this epistle 'our' refers to Paul together with the Corinthian *ecclesia*. Then, not all the city of Corinth, but those called out of it, even as saith the Lord at the beginning, 'I have much people in this city', Acts 18:10.

Not, I have the whole population of this city; but, 'I have much people'– out of the population –'in this city'. For the sins of these, Christ had died, as it is written by Paul the apostle to the *ecclesia* at Corinth, 'Christ died for *our* sins according to the scriptures', I Corinthians 15:3.

But what is a death 'according to the scriptures'? It is a sacrificial death; a substitutionary death; an atoning death; and it is an effectual death, all to put away sin by the sacrifice of himself.

It is a death depicted in the burnt offering, the meat offering, the peace offering, and the sin offering; in Abel's lamb and Abraham's ram; in the continual burnt offering; in the passover lamb; in the sacrifice of *Yom Kippur*, the day of atonement: *that* kind of death.

It is a death 'according to the scriptures' as saith the holy prophets which have been since the world began.

For example, the prophet Isaiah: he prophesied of a death 'according to the scriptures' saying, 'Surely he hath borne our griefs, and carried our sorrows: yet we did esteem him stricken, smitten of God, and afflicted. But he was wounded for our transgressions, he was bruised for our iniquities: the chastisement of our peace was upon him; and with his stripes we are healed.

'All we like sheep have gone astray; we have turned every one to his own way; and the LORD hath laid on him the iniquity of us all.'

And again, 'for the transgression of my people was he stricken.' Once more, 'by his knowledge shall my righteous servant justify many; for he shall bear their iniquities', Isaiah 53:4-6,8,11.

Now, this is a death, a substitutionary, sacrificial death, a death 'according to the scriptures'.

In that 'Christ died for our sins according to the scriptures', this does not mean some general, universal atonement effectual only when the will of man makes it applicable. On the contrary, it means a precise, particular atonement, in which he *actually took away the sins of those for whom he died at the moment at which he died.*

His shed blood was witness that *those sins were actually taken away for ever*: 'covered' by the blood, never again to appear before the righteous judgment and all-searching eye of Almighty God. They were gone for ever, *then*.

Hence the apostle stresses positively, 'Christ died for *our* sins according to the scriptures' for it is certain that all those for whom he died—including Paul and the *ecclesia* at Corinth—had their sins blotted out by the blood of Christ, when that blood was shed in death.

Hence Jesus saith 'This is my blood of the new testament, which is shed for many for the remission of sins', Matthew 26:28. Where notice, first, that it is the blood that was shed that remits the sins, not the believing upon it. What is believed upon is that *the blood, once shed, actually remitted, dismissed, those sins at that time.*

And, secondly, Jesus himself limits the application of the shed blood to the sins of 'many', a word which could only have been used because he deemed it necessary to qualify the number, lest any should suppose 'all'. Now, they cannot. Not for sins. Sin is another question.

As to sins, all those whose sins are forgiven them *had those sins blotted out when Jesus' blood was shed*. It was shed 'for the remission of sins', namely, of the 'many' in and under the new testament.

14

This is confirmed in the epistle to the Hebrews, where the writer affirms 'Christ was once offered to bear the sins of *many*', Hebrews 9:28. Here the sins, laid upon Christ, were *borne*, and, if so, borne *away*.

When? When 'Christ was once offered', namely, at the cross.

Whose sins? 'the sins of *many*', that is, of all those redeemed to God by the blood of the Lamb *out of* every kindred, and tongue, and people and nation, Revelation 5:9.

From which reference, notice, *blood* redeemed them, the blood of the Lamb, *when he was slain*, Revelation 5:9.

It is *this* that is meant, and to which the Holy Ghost bears witness, when it is said, 'Christ died for *our* sins according to the scriptures'.

By 'scriptures' in this place the apostle refers to the thirty-nine books of the old testament. But since the reference is apostolic, and in writing, it is proper to include the twenty-seven books of the new testament, given by the pen of the holy apostles after the ascension of the Lord Jesus, and following the descent of the Holy Ghost, who 'led them into all truth' besides 'bringing all things to their remembrance'.

Thus he embraces the entire inspired record of the books of the new testament, to be included–as implied–under the term 'scriptures', even as Peter testified of Paul's writings, counting them all of one with the 'other' scriptures, namely, the entire old testament, II Peter 3:16.

'And that he was buried', I Corinthians 15:4. 'And when they had fulfilled all that was written of him, they took him down, and laid him in a sepulchre', Acts 13:29.

This confirms his death with a witness: 'But when they came to Jesus, and saw that he was dead already, they brake not his legs:

but one of the soldiers with a spear pierced his side, and forthwith came there out blood and water.' 'Then took they the body of Jesus, and wound it in linen clothes with the spices, as the manner of the Jews is to bury', John 19:33,34,40.

From thence, they 'beheld the sepulchre, and how his body was laid', Luke 23:55.

'For', saith Jesus, 'as Jonas was three days and three nights in the belly of the great fish; so shall the Son of man be three days and three nights in the heart of the earth', Matthew 12:40.

Yet though his corpse was removed from the face of the earth, his dead body wrapped in grave clothes in the depths of the sepulchre, mute witness by its absence to all that had been taken away in death, yet he saw no corruption. 'Because thou wilt not leave my soul in *hadēs*, neither wilt thou suffer thine Holy One to see corruption.'

Where David, being a prophet, spake not of himself, but of Christ, 'that *his* soul was not left in *hadēs*, neither *his* flesh did see corruption', Acts 2:27,31. This word of Peter, quoting David, was given on the day of Pentecost.

Paul later confirms the same, saying, 'Thou shalt not suffer thine Holy One to see corruption', Acts 13:35 – no, not *see* corruption – even though his dead body lay in the grave those three days and three nights 'according to the scriptures'. This was attested by many witnesses, not only of his own disciples; but of the Roman authorities; their soldiers; the centurion; and the rulers and people of the Jewish nation.

'And that he rose again the third day according to the scriptures', I Corinthians 15:4. Of the resurrection from the dead, Peter testified on behalf of all the apostles: 'And we are witnesses of all things which he did both in the land of the Jews, and in Jerusalem; *whom they slew and hanged on a tree.*' That was what *they* did.

'Him God raised up the third day, and showed him openly; not to all the people, but unto witnesses chosen before of God, even to us, who did eat and drink with him *after he rose from the dead.*' And that was what God did. Acts 10:39-41.

Paul shows how the resurrection on the third day was 'according to the scriptures', declaring 'But God raised him from the dead', adding, 'And we declare unto you glad tidings, how that the promise which was made unto the fathers'—according to the scriptures—'God hath fulfilled the same unto us their children, *in that he hath raised up Jesus again;*

'As it is also written'—apart from the promise in the scriptures, 'also' the following prophecies appear in the psalms—'in the second psalm, Thou art my Son, this day have I begotten thee'—that is, from the *dead*. This day? Which day? The third day, 'according to the scriptures'.

'And as concerning that he raised him up from the dead'— according to the scriptures—'now no more to return to corruption, he saith on this wise, I will give you the sure mercies of David. Wherefore he saith also in another psalm, Thou shalt not suffer thine Holy One to see corruption.

'For David, after he had served his own generation by the will of God, fell on sleep, and was laid unto his fathers, and saw corruption: but he, *whom God raised again*, saw no corruption', Acts 13:30,32-37.

If this be not 'according to the scriptures' what is according to the scriptures? Here is a promise to the fathers, repeated again and again over the entire old testament. Further to which Paul quotes two psalms of David, and yet another insight into the future, to behold the resurrection from the dead, foretold by the prophet Isaiah.

And, remark, it is Jesus' *body* that was raised: he was raised *bodily*. His *body*—which in the case of all humanity save his, upon burial, saw corruption – 'as in Adam *all* die'; 'he was laid unto his fathers, and saw corruption' – the *same* body, this *same* Jesus, was physically raised from the dead, never having seen corruption, for ever to reign in life far beyond the reach of the grave, the other side of death.

That was the reality which gripped the apostles.

'Behold my hands and my feet, that *it is I myself*' – it is *the same body: the marks show it* – 'handle me, and see; for a spirit hath not *flesh and bones, as ye see me have*', Luke 24:39.

Likewise Jesus, risen *in the body*, the *same* body, the marks of the crucifixion upon him, saith to Thomas, 'Reach hither thy finger, and behold my hands; and reach hither thy hand, and thrust it into my side: and be not faithless, but believing', John 20:27.

That is, believing *in the resurrection of the same body, as such, from the grave in which he had been laid in death three days and three nights before.*

This was the truth, the astounding truth, the truth that vindicated Christ's coming, his life, his words, his death, his burial, all that had been achieved in death, every ancient prophecy that had passed upon him, his future glory, and his coming judgment.

'Because he' – God – 'hath appointed a day, in the which he will judge the world in righteousness by that man whom he hath ordained; whereof he hath given assurance unto all men, *in that he hath raised him from the dead*', Acts 17:31.

This, I say, *this* was the reality that gripped the apostles: *they were witnesses of his resurrection from the dead.*

'And as they spake unto the people, the priests, and the captain of the temple, and the Sadducees, came upon them, being grieved that they taught the people, and preached through Jesus the resurrection from the dead', Acts 4:1,2. 'And with great power gave the apostles witness of the resurrection of the Lord Jesus: and great grace was upon them all', Acts 4:33.

From the beginning this astounding verity, witnessed by their own eyes, ears, and hands, *gripped the apostles*. There *was* a resurrection of the dead, *witness the bodily resurrection of the Lord Jesus*.

'Whom God hath raised up, having loosed the pains of death: because it was not possible that he should be holden of it.

'For David speaketh concerning him'—his resurrection being according to the scriptures—'I foresaw the Lord always before my face, for he is on my right hand, that I should not be moved: therefore did my heart rejoice, and my tongue was glad; moreover also my flesh shall rest in hope:

'Because thou wilt not leave my soul in *hadēs*, neither wilt thou suffer thine Holy One to see corruption. Thou hast made known to me the ways of life; thou shalt make me full of joy with thy countenance.

'Men and brethren, let me freely speak unto you of the patriarch David, that he is both dead and buried, and his sepulchre is with us unto this day.

'Therefore being a prophet, and knowing that God had sworn with an oath unto him, that of the fruit of his loins, according to the flesh, he would raise up Christ to sit on his throne; he seeing this before spake'—and wrote in the scriptures some one thousand years before the event—'*of the resurrection of Christ,*

'That *his* soul'—not David's soul, who spoke and wrote of Christ a millennium before; but Christ's, of whom David prophesied—'*his* soul was not left in *hadēs*, neither *his* flesh did see corruption. This Jesus hath God raised up, whereof we all are witnesses'; so testified Peter on the day of Pentecost, Acts 2:24-32.

'And that he was *seen* of Cephas, then of the twelve: after that, he was *seen* of above five hundred brethren at once; of whom the greater part remain unto this present, but some are fallen asleep.

'After that, he was *seen* of James; then of all the apostles. And last of all he was *seen* of me also, as of one born out of due time', I Corinthians 15:5-8.

Now here are the holy apostles, chosen of God as eyewitnesses, impeccable in their truthfulness; here are above five hundred just, holy, and true brethren at once, most living when Paul wrote; here is James, a very pillar of rectitude; and here Paul himself, whose witness is true, and ye know that he speaks truth.

These all testify with one voice – the voice of unimpeachable honesty, and that by the Holy Ghost – not to add the voices of David and Isaiah, some one thousand years before, verified in the event – *one voice, I say, that, bodily, in the body in which he was crucified, witness the marks in his hands, feet, and side, bodily Jesus rose from the dead.*

And these all, seeing both it and him with their own eyes, speak to the ends of the world of what they witnessed infallibly, declaring the truth by the Holy Ghost from heaven.

Then, 'How say some among you that there is no resurrection of the dead?', I Corinthians 15:12.

How? For by so doing you make a lie of that evangel of which the apostle had shown – and *is* showing – *that the resurrection is an integral part*; you make a lie of the testimony of the Holy Ghost, who records that he rose from the dead, and bears record to this day; you make God a liar, who declares that he raised Christ from the dead; you make the Son of God a liar, who showed himself alive after his passion by many infallible proofs.

Moreover, you set aside as worth nothing more than a pack of lies the eyewitness of all the holy apostles, of Cephas, James, Paul himself, and above five hundred brethren at once.

And, despising so great a testimony as this, of God and man; heaven and earth; time and eternity; life and death; this world and the next; of all the apostles and five hundred brethren: I say to you, Tell us: Who are you?

Who do you think you are, and what have you seen, or what do you know? or how will the balance go, you laid on the one side, and this infallible, irrefutable, incontrovertible testimony, with all those who bore witness, on the other side?

'How say some among you that there is no resurrection of the dead?'

Next the apostle writes about himself, 'as one born out of due time'. The meaning is that as an *apostle* he did not come forth when he should have done. Thus he employs a kind of irony against himself, depreciating his apostleship in relation to the twelve.

'For I am the least of the apostles, that am not meet to be called an apostle, because'– before he was so called –'I persecuted the church of God', I Corinthians 15:9.

The twelve were called by the Son of man on earth in Israel, during the days of his flesh; Paul was called afterwards outside Damascus by the Son of God from heaven when he had entered into his glory.

But if this was the will of him who called every one of the apostles, who is he that shall require him to give an account of his matters?

For, saith Paul, '*By the grace of* God I am what I am: and his grace which was bestowed upon me was not in vain; but I laboured more abundantly than they all: yet not I, but the grace of God which was with me.

'Therefore, whether it were I or they, *so we preach, and so ye believed*', I Corinthians 15:10,11.

SECOND; THE INDISPENSABILITY OF THE TRUTH OF THE RESUR-RECTION TO THE INTEGRITY OF THE EVANGEL ENFORCED AGAINST THOSE WHO ERRED AT CORINTH, I CORINTHIANS 15:12.

Now here is the explanation for the apostle's emphasis on the evangel which he preached at the beginning in Corinth; of his recalling their reception of it; of the necessity of their continuing in it; of salvation being exclusive to it; and of his defining so clearly the very essence of the evangel itself; and, finally, besides all this, leading up to the explanation for the first four verses, the names and number of the witnesses of the resurrection of Christ from the dead, verses 4-11.

But what is the explanation? why all this? Because 'some among you' denied the resurrection of the dead, verse 12.

That is the reason for the earlier passage: *no one can deny the resurrection without denying the evangel in its essence.* It was *that* which the apostle had established in the opening verses.

As to them, where were the 'some' among them at the beginning? Then, all as one man had received the evangel, the whole evangel, and nothing but the evangel, preached by the apostle sent to them, verse 1.

And where were the 'some among you' in the interval? Not apparent until now? Indeed, there were not 'some' apart from 'all', at the beginning; nor, presumably, until comparatively recently.

For 'all' received the *whole* evangel at the first.

It was that 'wherein ye stand', and had stood up until now, namely, until 'some among you' fell away from the truth and in effect denied their standing: and openly, too, having no shame about 'saying' what denied both resurrection and evangel.

But let them be under no delusion: they were denying their own salvation: 'by which also ye are saved.'

But 'some among you' had forsaken that evangel, the rather inviting perdition than embracing salvation.

One must constantly recall the evangel, if one is to be saved at last: 'by which also ye are saved *if* ye keep in memory what I preached unto you', verse 1.

But they, the 'some', had expunged from their memories the integrity of the evangel, and, if so, these preferred erroneous heresies, apparently having believed in vain.

Was it so? Was it true that some had come to this: 'unless ye have believed in vain'? If not, 'How say some among you that there is no resurrection of the dead?', verse 12.

Note therefore the strength behind the opening words of the twelfth verse: 'Now if Christ be preached that he rose from the dead.'

If he be preached? But he was so preached! Such preaching was integral to the essence, the most basic truth of the evangel, as had been shown.

'For I delivered unto you first of all that which I also received, how that Christ died for our sins according to the scriptures; and that he was buried, and that he rose again the third day according to the scriptures', verses 3,4.

This *was* the preaching of the evangel. It was *the evangel itself*. Then why '*If* Christ be preached that he rose from the dead', verse 12?

For there *are* no 'ifs' or 'buts'. Christ *was* so preached. Yes, and at that preached by whom? By the holy apostles. Namely, by the eyewitnesses chosen of God.

By Cephas; by the twelve; by James. After that, by all the apostles, confirmed by above five hundred brethren at once.

And, finally, preached by Paul also, even as he clearly testified: 'Moreover, brethren, I declare unto you the evangel which I evangelized unto you.'

Then, these things being so, and they were so, 'how say some among you'–how *can* you say it? how *dare* you say it?–'that there is no resurrection of the dead?', I Corinthians 15:12. What is this but 'they that observe lying vanities forsake their own mercy', Jonah 2:8?

THIRD; THE DISASTROUS EFFECT UPON THE INTEGRITY OF THE EVANGEL RESULTING FROM THE DENIAL OF THE RESURRECTION, I CORINTHIANS 15:13-19.

In this passage the apostle reproves and convicts those who denied the resurrection of the dead despite their erstwhile confession of that evangel which they had heard and received in the beginning. Then, at the present, 'How say some among you that there is no resurrection of the dead?'.

This denied their first faith.

Moreover, such an appalling error – once granted – would result in disastrous consequences. Five disastrous consequences. Very well then, let them consider what they are saying:

First; if they were right 'that there is not a resurrection of the dead'–for so the Greek reads: it was not simply Christ's resurrection that they denied; they were saying *that there is not a resurrection of the dead at all*–then, if so, it must follow of necessity *that neither had Christ risen from the dead!*

'If there be no resurrection of the dead, then is *Christ* not risen', I Corinthians 15:13. Or, to render the Greek grammatical form, 'But if a resurrection of [the] dead there is not, *neither has Christ been raised.*'

In a word, Paul is saying, Unless *all* the dead rise, then *none* rise. Conversely, if *one* rose from the dead, then *all* must rise from the dead.

As sure as if *one* be born of woman, *all* are born of woman, and as certain as if *one* die, so *all* die – these things being immutable certainties – *so also is the resurrection*: if *one* rose, *all* will rise.

And who is he that can contend against the universal and immutable verities of the birth and death of all mankind? Then let none contend against the concomitant truth of the resurrection, attested by many infallible proofs witnessed of the one man, Christ Jesus. For if *all* rise not, 'then is *Christ* not risen', verse 13. But verses 4-8 show that Christ *is* risen. Then *all* shall rise, and there *is* – and must be – a universal resurrection of the dead.

Second; if they were right – God forbid – 'that there is not a resurrection of the dead', then Christ could not have risen: for, as Paul had shown, either the dead rise, or the dead rise not. And if *all* the dead rise not, then *none* of the dead rise.

As certainly as the birth of *one* man attests the birth of *all* men; and as surely as the death of *one* man presages the death of *all* men, so infallibly does the resurrection of *one* ensure the resurrection of *all*. For it is no more ludicrous in the face of *one* resurrection to deny the resurrection of *all*, than it is in the birth and death of *one* man to conclude that these events are not common to the whole of mankind.

Now let those who say that there is no resurrection consider what they do. One, they make the apostles' preaching vain, verse 14, or, as the Greek has it, 'then void is our proclamation'.

25

Obviously: for the apostles proclaimed the opposite to that which these affirmed. The apostles preached the truth of the resurrection and the judgment to come, namely, that God 'hath given assurance unto all men, in that he hath raised him' – the man Christ Jesus – 'from the dead', Acts 17:31.

But these said, 'there is no resurrection of the dead'. And, if not, 'then is our preaching vain'. Two, 'and your faith is also vain', I Corinthians 15:14.

That is, such 'faith' as remained to them, after they had lacerated the truth, and left the evangel in tatters. What 'faith' was that? Well, that *somehow* Jesus still loved them, and *one way or another* they would be forgiven. The apostle calls this 'vain'. Vain faith. Or, as the Greek has it, 'and void also is your faith'. It will not, and it cannot, save.

Three, 'Yea, and we are found false witnesses of God; because we have testified of God that he raised up Christ: *whom he raised not up, if so be that the dead rise not.*'

Then, are we liars, or are they liars? Do we make God a liar, or do they make God a liar? One or the other is true.

And this also is true: if *one* man rises, all men rise. If all men rise not, no man rises. But we testify of God that he *did* raise one man, Christ Jesus. This, they contradict by denying the resurrection of all men: 'whom he raised not up, if the dead rise not', I Corinthians 15:15.

Third; if they were right – God forbid – 'that there is not a resurrection of the dead' then it must be true after all that Christ rose not: for it is certain that he died, yea, was both dead and buried. 'For if the dead rise not, then is not Christ raised', I Corinthians 15:16.

Where either *man as such rises*, or, *man as such does not rise*. And, if but *one* man rose, then *all* must rise. But these said 'the dead rise not', and, if not, 'then is not Christ risen'.

26

If not, then *who* was it that so many and such impeccable eyewitnesses both handled and saw? 'That which we have *seen* and *heard* declare we unto you, that ye also may have fellowship with us: and truly our fellowship is with the Father, and with his Son Jesus Christ', I John 1:3.

Fourth; if they were right 'that there is not a resurrection of the dead', three things must follow: one, their faith is vain. There is nothing to believe, because nothing is corroborated.

Indeed, since Christ plainly taught that he would rise again on the third day, then *nothing* that he said, and *nothing* that he did, can be believed, *if that failed to happen*. Then, their faith is vain.

Two, they are yet in their sins. Even *if* they believed that he took their sins upon himself *in* death, and yet *after* death rose not, evidently he took them not *away*.

Resurrection was the witness, the only possible witness, that his death was effectual before God to take away sins; which he took not away, if he rose not: 'ye are yet in your sins.'

Three, all those who died in faith, with all those who have since fallen asleep in Christ, died and fell asleep under a delusion: if *he* rose not, it is certain that *they* will not rise.

Hence, observe the consequences 'if Christ be not raised'. One: 'your faith is vain'. Two: 'ye are yet in your sins'. And three: 'then they which are fallen asleep in Christ are perished', I Corinthians 15:17,18.

Fifth; if–God forbid–they were right 'that there is not a resurrection of the dead', then yet three further things follow of necessity.

One, we have no hope in this life. Fearful, black, unknown terrors face us the moment we die: in view of *that*, this present life is filled with hopelessness.

Two, neither have we any hope in the life to come. Since there was nothing to give us hope under the sun in the land of the living, what hope can there be under the blackness of darkness in the unending world of lost souls into which we must pass immediately upon death?

Three, knowing this, unable – unlike the vain fools – to forget such things for one single moment, then, through fear of death, we are all our lifetime subject to bondage.

This brings down the old yoke; it lays us under an intolerable burden; it binds us hand and foot with the chains of horror; and it shuts fast the two leaved gate beyond recovery.

In a word, 'If in this life only we have hope' – and even had we *this* fleeting relief, knowing what we do of the fearful terrors that await us beyond the grave, then – 'we are of all men most miserable', I Corinthians 15:19.

FOURTH; THE INDISPENSABILITY OF THE TRUTH OF THE RESUR-RECTION TO THE REALIZATION OF THE COUNSEL AND PURPOSE OF GOD, I CORINTHIANS 15:20-28.

'But now is Christ risen from the dead, and become the first-fruits of them that slept', I Corinthians 15:20. 'But' – as opposed to all the cavilling of every disputer in the whole world: in contrast, *but* – 'now *is* Christ risen from the dead.'

Now? When? 'the third day according to the scriptures', verse 4. Consider that day; consider the signs on that day:

'There was a great earthquake: for the angel of the Lord descended from heaven, and came and rolled back the stone from the door, and sat upon it. His countenance was like light-ning, and his raiment white as snow: and for fear of him the keepers did shake, and became as dead men.

'And the angel answered and said unto the women, Fear not ye: for I know that ye seek Jesus, which was crucified. He is not here: for he is risen, as he said. Come, see the place where the Lord lay. And go quickly, and tell his disciples that he is risen from the dead; and, behold, he goeth before you into Galilee; there shall ye see him: lo, I have told you.

'And they departed quickly from the sepulchre with fear and great joy; and did run to bring his disciples word. And as they went to tell his disciples, behold, Jesus met them, saying, All hail.

'And they came and held him by the feet, and worshipped him. Then said Jesus unto them, Be not afraid: go tell my brethren that they go into Galilee, and there shall they see me', Matthew 28:2-10.

'Then the eleven disciples went away into Galilee, into a mountain where Jesus had appointed them. And when they saw him, they worshipped him: but some doubted.

'And Jesus came and spake unto them, saying, All power is given unto me in heaven and in earth. Go ye therefore, and teach all nations, baptizing them in the name of the Father, and of the Son, and of the Holy Ghost: teaching them to observe all things whatsoever I have commanded you:

'And, lo, I am with you alway, even unto the end of the world', Matthew 28:16-20.

Once more: 'And when the sabbath was past, Mary Magdalene, and Mary the mother of James, and Salome, had brought sweet spices, that they might come and anoint him. And very early in the morning the first day of the week, they came unto the sepulchre at the rising of the sun.

'And they said among themselves, Who shall roll us away the stone from the door of the sepulchre? And when they looked, they saw that the stone was rolled away: for it was very great.

'And entering into the sepulchre, they saw a young man sitting on the right side, clothed in a long white garment; and they were affrighted.

'And he saith unto them, Be not affrighted: Ye seek Jesus of Nazareth, which was crucified: he is risen; he is not here: behold the place where they laid him. But go your way, tell his disciples and Peter that he goeth before you into Galilee: there shall ye see him, as he said unto you', Mark 16:1-7.

'Now when Jesus was risen early the first day of the week, he appeared first to Mary Magdalene, out of whom he had cast seven devils', Mark 16:9.

'After that he appeared in another form unto two of them, as they walked, and went into the country', Mark 16:12.

'Afterwards he appeared unto the eleven as they sat at meat', Mark 16:14.

'And he said unto them, Go ye into all the world, and preach the gospel to every creature. He that believeth and is baptized shall be saved; but he that believeth not shall be damned', Mark 16:15,16.

'So then after the Lord had spoken unto them, he was received up into heaven, and sat on the right hand of God. And they went forth, and preached everywhere, the Lord working with them, and confirming the word with signs following. Amen', Mark 16:19,20.

And again: 'Now upon the first day of the week, very early in the morning, they came unto the sepulchre, bringing the spices which they had prepared, and certain others with them. And they found the stone rolled away from the sepulchre. And they entered in, and found not the body of the Lord Jesus.

'And it came to pass, as they were much perplexed thereabout, behold, two men stood by them in shining garments:

and as they were afraid, and bowed down their faces to the earth, they said unto them, Why seek ye the living among the dead?

'He is not here, but is risen: remember how he spake unto you when he was yet in Galilee, saying, The Son of man must be delivered into the hands of sinful men, and be crucified, and the third day rise again', Luke 24:1-7.

'And, behold, two of them went that same day to a village called Emmaus, which was from Jerusalem about threescore furlongs. And they talked together of all these things which had happened. And it came to pass, that, while they communed together and reasoned, Jesus himself drew near, and went with them.

'But their eyes were holden that they should not know him', Luke 24:13-16.

'Then he said unto them, O fools, and slow of heart to believe all that the prophets have spoken: Ought not Christ to have suffered these things, and to enter into his glory?

'And beginning at Moses and all the prophets, he expounded unto them in all the scriptures the things concerning himself. And they drew nigh unto the village, whither they went: and he made as though he would have gone further.

'But they constrained him, saying, Abide with us: for it is toward evening, and the day is far spent. And he went in to tarry with them. And it came to pass, as he sat at meat with them, he took bread, and blessed it, and brake, and gave to them. And their eyes were opened, and they knew him; and he vanished out of their sight.

'And they said one to another, Did not our heart burn within us, while he talked with us by the way, and while he opened to us the scriptures?

'And they rose up the same hour, and returned to Jerusalem, and found the eleven gathered together, and them that were with them, saying, The Lord is risen indeed, and hath appeared to Simon.

'And they told what things were done in the way, and how he was known of them in breaking of bread. And as they thus spake, Jesus himself stood in the midst of them, and saith unto them, Peace be unto you.

'But they were terrified and affrighted, and supposed that they had seen a spirit.

'And he said unto them, Why are ye troubled? and why do thoughts arise in your hearts? Behold my hands and my feet, that it is I myself: handle me, and see; for a spirit hath not flesh and bones, as ye see me have.

'And when he had thus spoken, he showed them his hands and his feet.

'And while they yet believed not for joy, and wondered, he said unto them, Have ye here any meat? And they gave him a piece of a broiled fish, and of an honeycomb. And he took it, and did eat before them.

'And he said unto them, These are the words which I spake unto you, while I was yet with you, that all things must be fulfilled, which were written in the law of Moses, and in the prophets, and in the psalms, concerning me.

'Then opened he their understanding, that they might understand the scriptures, and said unto them, Thus it is written, and thus it behoved Christ to suffer, and to rise from the dead the third day: and that repentance and remission of sins should be preached in his name among all nations, beginning at Jerusalem.

'And ye are witnesses of these things', Luke 24:25-48.

'And he led them out as far as to Bethany, and he lifted up his hands, and blessed them. And it came to pass, while he blessed them, he was parted from them, and carried up into heaven', Luke 24:50,51.

Yet again: 'Mary stood without at the sepulchre weeping: and as she wept, she stooped down, and looked into the sepulchre, and seeth two angels in white sitting, the one at the head, and the other at the feet, where the body of Jesus had lain.

'And they say unto her, Woman, why weepest thou? She saith unto them, Because they have taken away my Lord, and I know not where they have laid him.

'And when she had thus said, she turned herself back, and saw Jesus standing, and knew not that it was Jesus.

'Jesus saith unto her, Woman, why weepest thou? whom seekest thou? She, supposing him to be the gardener, saith unto him, Sir, if thou have borne him hence, tell me where thou hast laid him, and I will take him away.

'Jesus saith unto her, Mary. She turned herself, and saith unto him, Rabboni; which is to say, Master.

'Jesus saith unto her, Touch me not; for I am not yet ascended to my Father: but go to my brethren, and say unto them, I ascend unto my Father, and your Father; and to my God, and your God', John 20:11-17.

'Then the same day at evening, being the first day of the week, when the doors were shut where the disciples were assembled for fear of the Jews, came Jesus and stood in the midst, and saith unto them, Peace be unto you. And when he had so said, he showed unto them his hands and his side.

'Then were the disciples glad, when they saw the Lord. Then said Jesus to them again, Peace be unto you: as my Father hath sent me, even so send I you.

'And when he had said this, he breathed on them, and saith unto them, Receive ye the Holy Ghost: whose soever sins ye remit, they are remitted unto them; and whose soever sins ye retain, they are retained.

'But Thomas, one of the twelve, called Didymus, was not with them when Jesus came. The other disciples therefore said unto him, We have seen the Lord. But he said unto them, Except I shall see in his hands the print of the nails, and put my finger into the print of the nails, and thrust my hand into his side, I will not believe.

'And after eight days again his disciples were within, and Thomas with them: then came Jesus, the doors being shut, and stood in the midst, and said, Peace be unto you.

'Then saith he to Thomas, Reach hither thy finger, and behold my hands; and reach hither thy hand, and thrust it into my side: and be not faithless, but believing. And Thomas answered and said unto him, My Lord and my God.

'Jesus saith unto him, Thomas, because thou hast seen me, thou hast believed: blessed are they that have not seen, and yet have believed', John 20:11-29.

Moreover the Acts of the Apostles records the great power with which the eleven gave testimony to the resurrection of the Lord Jesus. For example, in the opening words the writer looks back on the ministry of the Lord, declaring 'all that Jesus began both to do and teach'.

Then, again, he looks forward to his risen administration from the glory, the other side of death, affirming that 'he was taken up, after that he through the Holy Ghost had given commandments unto the apostles whom he had chosen:

'To whom also he showed himself alive after his passion by many infallible proofs, being seen of them forty days, and speaking of the things pertaining to the kingdom of God', Acts 1:1-3.

'And when he had spoken these things, while they beheld, he was taken up; and a cloud received him out of their sight', Acts 1:9.

'This Jesus hath God raised up, whereof we all are witnesses', Acts 2:32.

'Unto you first God, having raised up his Son Jesus, sent him to bless you, in turning away every one of you from his iniquities', Acts 3:26.

But 'as they spake unto the people, the priests, and the captain of the temple, and the Sadducees, came upon them, being grieved that they taught the people, and preached through Jesus the resurrection from the dead', Acts 4:1,2.

Boldly the apostles testified that which they had seen, in the power which they had received, namely, 'Jesus Christ of Nazareth, whom ye crucified, whom God raised from the dead', Acts 4:10.

So that 'with great power gave the apostles witness of the resurrection of the Lord Jesus: and great grace was upon them all', Acts 4:33.

Hence Peter declared on behalf of all the apostles, 'And we are witnesses of all things which he did both in the land of the Jews, and in Jerusalem; whom they slew and hanged on a tree: him God raised up the third day, and showed him openly; not to all the people, but unto witnesses chosen before of God, even to us, who did eat and drink with him after he rose from the dead.

'And he commanded us to preach unto the people, and to testify that it is he which was ordained of God to be the Judge of quick and dead', Acts 10:39-42.

But there was one born out of due time, the last of the apostles, who saw him not as did Peter and the others, on earth, but uniquely, in heaven, whence the apostle Paul was called to the apostolate from the heights of glory:

'And it came to pass, that, as I made my journey, and was come nigh unto Damascus about noon, suddenly there shone from heaven a great light round about me. And I fell unto the ground, and heard a voice saying unto me, Saul, Saul, why persecutest thou me?

'And I answered, Who art thou, Lord?

'And he said unto me, I am Jesus of Nazareth, whom thou persecutest', Acts 22:6-8.

No wonder therefore that central to the evangel sounded forth the testimony of Paul the apostle before all the Jewish religious authorities: 'But this I confess', declared he, 'that after the way which they call heresy, so worship I the God of my fathers, believing all things which are written in the law and in the prophets:

'And have hope toward God, which they themselves also allow, that there shall be a resurrection of the dead, both of the just and unjust', Acts 24:14,15.

Now Paul was not an eyewitness during the forty days in which Christ, risen from the dead, appeared to the eleven. Then how did he know of and bear witness to the resurrection?

Because *his first acquaintance with him with whom the other apostles ate and drank after he rose from the dead, was after he had ascended into heaven.*

Their last view of him was in the cloud that received him out of their sight when he was caught up to heaven as he ascended. *Paul's* first view of him was without a cloud after he had ascended into his glory, being sat down at the right hand of the Father.

But whether the eleven, or Paul, all the apostles as one man had this testimony: *he whom they saw was risen from the grave, the other side of death, alive for evermore in that very body in which he had been crucified, death defeated, the grave vanquished,* even as saith the Lord from the glory of heaven to the last of the apostles: '*I am Jesus.*'

If so, not only risen, not in the act of ascending, but seated in glorious exaltation at the right hand of the Father. *In the body.* Then, it follows – it *must* follow – there *is* a resurrection of the dead.

'But *now* is Christ risen from the dead.' If *now* – a recurring present – how shall we know of the resurrection? In the same way as the Corinthians.

Yet, as they experienced, so do we: for all the *infallible* proofs; for all the *impeccable* eyewitnesses; for all the *immutability* of the scriptures: until our blinded hearts are enlightened; until our darkened minds are illuminated, until God, who commanded the light to shine out of darkness, shines in our hearts to give the light of the knowledge of the glory of God in the face of Jesus Christ, *we cannot believe.*

Now, however, God has opened the eyes of our understanding, and, behold, we *see.* Not as the chosen eyewitnesses saw, who saw literally, but, enlightened by the Father from heaven, receiving in *that* light the testimony of the holy apostles, *now we see spiritually.*

No less than they, we too are blessed, as saith Jesus, 'Blessed are they that have *not* seen, yet have *believed*', John 20:29.

Wherefore a vast multitude, whom no man can number, preceded us, but included us, *who also have seen spiritually, and believed,* as it is written, 'Whom having not seen, ye love; in whom, though now ye see him not, yet believing, ye rejoice with joy unspeakable and full of glory: receiving the end of your faith, even the salvation of your souls', I Peter 1:8,9.

This is that of which Jesus spake, saying, 'This is the will of him that sent me, *that every one which seeth the Son,* and'—in consequence of this *seeing*—'believeth on him, may have everlasting life: and I will raise him up at the last day', John 6:40.

Of this inward, spiritual *seeing*, in consequence of which the light shines on and through the apostolic eyewitness, one can say, 'But *now* is Christ risen from the dead', because every one of those in the secret declares from the heart, 'One thing I know, that, whereas I was blind, now I see', John 9:25.

This *seeing* the world receiveth not, though outwardly and formally it may profess the record of the eyewitnesses.

It may: but it is sightless, and in the dark, and, whatever the profession, it is not that of saving faith, as saith Jesus, 'The world seeth me no more'.

No, the world seeth him no more, but to those illuminated by the Father, he saith, '*but ye see me*: because I live, ye shall live also', John 14:19.

'But *now* is Christ risen from the dead', I Corinthians 15:20.

'And become the firstfruits of them that slept.' The term 'firstfruits' refers to an old testament figure typical of Christ in relation to his people.

The expression 'them that slept' indicates all those who ever have, or ever will, 'fall asleep', that is, die in the faith of Christ, having been laid to rest in union with him.

As to their bodies, even to this very generation, having 'fallen asleep', these sleep on.

But the 'firstfruits' does not sleep on. He is risen: 'But now is Christ risen from the dead.'

In relation to the *bodies* of the sleepers in Christ, though sleeping still, the promise of the harvest is certain in the first-fruits: 'But now is Christ risen from the dead, *and become the firstfruits of them that slept*', I Corinthians 15:20.

'Seven weeks shalt thou number unto thee: begin to number the seven weeks from such time as thou beginnest to put the sickle to the corn', Deuteronomy 16:9.

'And thou shalt observe the feast of weeks, of the firstfruits of wheat harvest.' 'The first of the firstfruits of thy land thou shalt bring unto the house of the LORD thy God', Exodus 34:22,26.

'When ye be come into the land which I give unto you, and shall reap the harvest thereof, then shall ye bring a sheaf'– observe: *one* sheaf–'of the firstfruits of your harvest unto the priest: and he shall wave the sheaf before the LORD, to be accepted for you: on the morrow after the sabbath'–mark that: *on the morrow after the sabbath* –'the priest shall wave it', Leviticus 23:10,11.

So that at the time the green ears of the wheat harvest just begin to ripen, then, here and there, in the most advantageous, sheltered, and sunny situations, an ear or two would appear golden ripe, in advance of and anticipating the whole harvest.

These relatively few advanced ears were cut off at the stalk from the ground and gathered together, a kind of witness of the whole harvest yet to come.

This sheaf, called the firstripe sheaf, was offered on 'the morrow after the sabbath'.

The cutting off of the firstripe sheaf from the earth answered to the day of the passover in the type, when Christ hung on the cross and was put to death: 'he was cut off out of the land of the living', Isaiah 53:8.

The morrow after the sabbath, namely, the first day of the week, this firstripe sheaf was waved by the priest before the LORD. In the figure, all the harvest was seen in him in his death and burial: 'he was cut off out of the land of the living: for the transgression of my people was he stricken', Isaiah 53:8.

Now, risen, severed from the earth, on the day of the resurrection, he appears as set forth wholly free of all root or connection with or in this present world, held up in priestly hands, waved in joy and triumph, an exultant demonstration *that nothing of the earth, or of the world, or of time, was in this victorious liberty before all the heavens.*

However, when the priest waved the firstripe sheaf, not only that sheaf in itself, but in those full and abundant ears *all the harvest was signified.*

'He shall wave *the*'–singular–'sheaf before the LORD, to be accepted for *you*'–plural; Leviticus 23:11.

From the day that the firstripe sheaf was waved the counting began. This counting ended forty-nine days later.

Of that last day it is written, 'When the day of Pentecost was fully come, they were all with one accord in one place. And suddenly there came a sound from heaven as of a rushing mighty wind, and it filled all the house where they were sitting.

'And there appeared unto them cloven tongues like as of fire, and it sat upon each of them. And they were all filled with the Holy Ghost', Acts 2:1-4.

This, the beginning of the *ecclesia*, and of the constitution of the body of Christ, was in itself significant of all who should be conformed to the image of God's Son, Romans 8:29.

If so, of the final harvest. A week of weeks, seven days seven times over – seven being the number symbolizing perfection – indicates perfection perfected.

Typified on the day of Pentecost, such perfect consummation has its true fulfilment in the reaping of the harvest at the last day.

Whatever was true of that firstripe sheaf, must be true of the whole harvest.

Hence, as the firstripe sheaf was carefully gathered by being put to the sickle, the harvest of that from which the firstripe sheaf was taken must likewise be reaped: 'And he that sat on the cloud thrust in his sickle on the earth; and the earth was reaped', Revelation 14:16.

'And he shall gather his wheat into the garner', Matthew 3:12. 'Gather the wheat into my barn', Matthew 13:30.

'The harvest is the end of the world', Matthew 13:39.

'But now is Christ risen from the dead, and become the first-fruits of them that slept', I Corinthians 15:20.

It is of the essence in I Corinthians 15:20-28 that one neither loses sight of the context, nor errs from the discipline of its constraints. The context is exclusive to the second man not the first; to the evangel not the law; to Zion not Sinai; to the resurrection of the just not of the wicked; to what is in Christ not what is in Adam; to the heavenly inheritance not the earthly; to the counsel of God and his purpose, not that of man or of this present world.

In context the apostle goes on to speak of the harvest of which Christ had been the firstfruits.

He does not speak of any other harvest; there is another, but he does not speak of it: that is not his subject. Here, he is concerned only with what pertains to Christ, namely that resurrection of which his own resurrection had been the harbinger.

It is the truth of the resurrection in Christ which constrains the apostle to reach upwards to the stupendous heights which culminate in the climax of verse 28: it is the indispensable truth of the resurrection in connection with the evangel: it is the resurrection *of the ecclesia.*

It is not a question of how that resurrection is a blessing to *us.* It is a question of what that resurrection brings in for God.

First and foremost, the evangel of Christ is not centred upon man: above all, what is in view is the glory of God. It is not *our* salvation; *our* service; *our* sanctification; *our* resurrection; *our* inheritance that is pre-eminent: all these things are subservient to the counsel, purpose, and glory of God, and find their significance in relation to *that.*

It is a question of 'what is the hope of *his* calling', and, 'what the riches of the glory of *his* inheritance in the saints', Ephesians 1:18.

The evangel is firstly *for* God: *his* will; *his* counsel; *his* purpose; *his* inheritance; *his* glory: *that* was foremost in the faith of Jesus Christ, and therefore in the evangel, and hence in the resurrection of the dead.

Therefore the reality of the resurrection of the just, of the *ecclesia,* of the harvest of which Christ was the firstfruits, brings to pass God's counsel and purpose. That is why Paul now sets forth for the instruction of the Corinthians the tremendous truths of verses 20-28.

'For since by man came death, by man came also the resurrection of the dead. For as in Adam all die, even so in Christ shall all be made alive', I Corinthians 15:21,22.

Whereas the first part of each of the two verses appears to be negative, this is not so in fact. Actually the apostle employs the truth of the judgment of God upon Adam and the dire consequences to the whole of his posterity as a contrasting figure of the very opposite that is true in Christ.

Whatever is negatively true of man in Adam, much more is the opposite positively true of man in Christ.

There are *two* men, and their respective seeds. It is imperative to grasp and hold this distinction. Likewise that what is true of each of the two, respectively–in consequence of their having acted on behalf of all those whom they begat–by a law of necessity becomes true of all those begotten by them.

Then, since 'by man'–the first man–'came death', the parallel holds good: 'by man'–the second man–'came also the resurrection of the dead.'

The resurrection of the dead? Yes, *to all those seen in himself and of himself, on whose behalf the second man acted, to whose account God reckons his action, and who are in consequence begotten in him.* And none other.

Then, since 'in Adam all die', a negative fact that cannot be controverted, equally–yea, how much more!–in the *last* Adam a positive consequence must follow to his posterity as surely as he himself rose from the dead.

That is, by a law of necessity, all *his* seed, on whose behalf he acted, who are begotten in him, *must become partakers of his actions*: in a word, 'even so in Christ shall all be made alive.'

It cannot be overstressed that in the will, counsel, purpose and creation of God there are *two* men, not one. The failure to perceive this makes confusion worse confounded and brings down darkness and obscurity upon the minds of men.

Hence the god of this world, who blinds the minds of them that believe not, exploits men's incredulity at such a distinction to the utmost. Then they will never see light.

The revelation that there is not only a first Adam, but also a last; that there is not only a first man, but likewise a second; *and that these are entirely distinct, as are those begotten from them; besides the consequences of their actions upon their respective seeds*: these are paramount truths that form the basis of Paul's argument in I Corinthians 15:20-28, and to a very much greater extent in Romans 5:12-21.

So that 'since by man came death', and, 'as in Adam all die', are not expressions employed by the apostle as negative discouragements to the Corinthians. On the contrary, what is true of Adam, the first man, is used to show that *exactly the opposite must be, and is, much more true of Christ, the second man, and, if of him, then of all his seed.*

Hence far from having a negative effect verses 20 and 21 redound to the glory of God in Christ, revealing a hidden mystery, a purpose from before the foundation of the world, utterly transcending the man of this world, the world itself, and all that happens in the world from its creation to its dissolution.

The glorious triumph of Christ for all those chosen in him from before the foundation of the world – and therefore before the creation of Adam – rings with the shout of victory and resounds again and again from one end of the vault of heaven to the other; from eternity across time to eternity; to echo for ever through everlasting ages in the fulfilment of the purpose of God in the glorious inheritance of the kingdom of our God, and of his Christ, world without end. Amen.

This is the prospect that Paul the apostle sets before the *ecclesia* at Corinth in the resurrection from the dead.

'But every man in his own order: Christ the firstfruits; afterward they that are Christ's at his coming', I Corinthians 15:23, where 'afterward' refers to the resurrection of 'they that are Christ's'—and, if so, of the *ecclesia* at Corinth—a resurrection precisely commensurate with the figure of the reaping of the whole harvest, seen in figure fifty days before, when the firstripe sheaf had been put to the sickle, reaped and waved before the LORD in priestly hands lifted up to heaven.

For just as surely as the whole harvest was seen in the firstfruits, so 'they that are Christ's'—having been counted as risen in his resurrection—must and shall rise again in due order 'at his coming' for the full harvest of all that are his own.

'Then cometh the end, when he shall have delivered up the kingdom to God, even the Father; when he shall have put down all rule and all authority and power', I Corinthians 15:24.

That is, following the resurrection—'*afterward* they that are Christ's at his coming'—'*then* cometh the end.' At this, Christ 'shall have delivered up the kingdom to God, even the Father', namely, delivered it up *as risen from the dead*.

Not only the *ecclesia*, but all the old testament saints, the Israel of God, all those who 'without us should not be made perfect', Hebrews 11:40. But now they are made perfect, perfect in one, perfect in the body of the resurrection, and so presented in perfection to God and the Father by the Son of his love.

This is called 'delivering up the kingdom', namely, the entire kingdom of the reign and dominion of Christ, called out from the foundation of the world to the end of it, brought to completion in the resurrection of the just.

And this is the consummation of the work of the Son throughout time, fulfilled in his incarnation, baptism, transfiguration, visitation, crucifixion, resurrection, ascension, and, at the last, in his coming again for his own.

'For the Lord himself shall descend from heaven with a shout, with the voice of the archangel, and with the trump of God: and the dead in Christ shall rise first: then we which are alive and remain shall be caught up together with them in the clouds, to meet the Lord in the air: and so shall we ever be with the Lord', I Thessalonians 4:16,17.

As to the use of the word 'kingdom', in 'when he shall have delivered up the kingdom to God, even the Father': whilst the subject is the resurrection of the *ecclesia*, nevertheless in that resurrection more is included, namely *all* 'they that are Christ's'.

This goes back to the foundation of the world, taking in the patriarchs and all the seed of promise, that is, all the old testament saints. These also are 'they that are Christ's', though they never saw the fulfilment of that in which they believed, nor experienced the constitution of the *ecclesia*, the body of Christ.

'These all died in faith, not having received the promises, but having seen them afar off, and were persuaded of them, and embraced them, and confessed that they were strangers and pilgrims on the earth', Hebrews 11:13.

What promises? Particularly, of the righteousness of faith through the death of the promised Messiah, and of the resurrection from the dead to an eternal inheritance. Then shall not these, equally with the *ecclesia*, at the coming of Christ and the resurrection of them that are his, be partakers of this better resurrection?

They shall indeed, for 'these all, having obtained a good report through faith, received not the promise: God having provided some better thing for us, that they without us should not be made perfect', Hebrews 11:39,40.

Hence in the visions recorded in the Book of the Revelation there are seen twenty-four elders on thrones about the throne of God in heaven, symbolic of the twelve patriarchs and of the twelve apostles, and, if so, of the old and new testament saints whom they represent.

Likewise, though the names of the twelve apostles are in the foundations of the holy city, nevertheless the names of the twelve patriarchs are in the gates, signifying that in the resurrection at the coming of Christ for his own, *all* his own, from the foundation of the world, old and new testament saints alike, shall rise from the dead at the shout, at the voice of the archangel, and at the trump of God.

Hence ancient Job could say, 'For I know that my redeemer liveth, and that he shall stand at the latter day upon the earth: and though after my skin worms destroy this body, yet in my flesh shall I see God: whom I shall see for myself, and mine eyes shall behold, and not another; though my reins be consumed within me', Job 19:25-27.

Similarly David could cry in prophecy a thousand years before the coming of Christ, proclaiming his resurrection, 'Yet have I set my king upon my holy hill of Zion. I will declare the decree: the LORD hath said unto me, Thou art my Son; this day have I begotten thee', Psalm 2:6,7.

Moreover the prophet proclaimed to Israel, 'Behold, thy King cometh unto thee', Zechariah 9:9.

And again, Isaiah crieth unto Zion, 'Thy God reigneth!', Isaiah 52:7.

Now all these died in faith, looking for a kingdom, that is, an heavenly, and neither shall any of these heirs of faith be disappointed when Christ comes again for *all* that are his at the resurrection of the dead, for, with the *ecclesia*, they shall be raised to an everlasting kingdom and inheritance.

But this kingdom came not with observation, Luke 17:20, though they had thought to observe it at the coming of Christ.

However then—and even until now—it is interior and spiritual, so that of the inward present reign of Christ we read, 'the kingdom of God is not meat and drink; but righteousness, and peace, and joy in the Holy Ghost', Romans 14:17.

At present it is inward: but at the last it shall be outward. Hence Christ taught his disciples to pray, 'Thy kingdom *come*'. That is, 'come' with the resurrection and bringing in of the everlasting inheritance.

But—before Pentecost—these two things were what the apostles confounded, asking, 'Lord, wilt thou at this time restore again the kingdom to Israel?', Acts 1:6.

For they were yet blinded by Jewish prejudices: the kingdom was ordained and promised long before Israel, though Israel in turn looked for it: but it came not with observation, yet was inwardly established in the saints, though it shall not be seen in its glory till Christ comes again and delivers up the kingdom to the Father following the resurrection and after the destruction of all his enemies.

Of this, the dying thief had a better view than the apostles before Pentecost, for he cried out to the Saviour, 'Lord, remember me when thou comest into thy kingdom', Luke 23:42.

The kingdom therefore, in its manifestation and glory, pertains to the resurrection and the world to come.

In one way or another, however, whether as looked for, believed in, hoped after, or as inwardly received, spiritually entered, or experienced in union, from the beginning of the world to the end of it, 'they that are Christ's' shall surely hear the good word of God at the resurrection of the dead from the King in his beauty in the land that is very far off.

'Then shall the King say unto them on his right hand, Come, ye blessed of my Father, inherit the kingdom prepared for you from the foundation of the world', Matthew 25:34.

And now from henceforth shall be brought to pass the saying that is written, 'The kingdoms of this world are become the kingdoms of our Lord, and of his Christ; and he shall reign for ever and ever', Revelation 11:15.

And again, 'And the angel said unto her, Fear not, Mary: for thou hast found favour with God. And, behold, thou shalt conceive in thy womb, and bring forth a son, and shalt call his name JESUS. He shall be great, and shall be called the Son of the Highest: and the Lord God shall give unto him the throne of his father David: and he shall reign over the house of Jacob for ever; and of his kingdom there shall be no end', Luke 1:30-33.

And this shall come to pass in its fulness when 'he shall have put down all rule and all authority and power', I Corinthians 15:24.

If so, the *present* rulers, and the *present* authorities, and the *present* powers, in this world and throughout time, *are not put down* on the one hand, but reign in authority and power under the heavens *against the kingdom and rule of the Son of God from the highest glory* on the other hand.

And these powers will *continue* their reign until he rises up from the throne of his Father who is Head over all, despite the adversaries in this present age, withal the enemies in their positions of vast authority, but, nevertheless, destined to be overthrown 'when he shall have put down all rule and all authority and power'.

'For he must reign'–that is, above all heavens, unseen and supreme, and, at that, despite the continued existence of the rule and authority and power at enmity far below–'he must reign, till he hath put all his enemies under his feet.

49

'The last enemy that shall be destroyed is death', I Corinthians 15:25,26.

If so, the earth, the world, the heavens, this present age, are all filled with and ruled by his *enemies*. In the beginning he appointed the lawfully ordained rule and authority and power, but, under the Adversary, these rebelled, and, from the Fall, brought down the darkness, and the reign of sin and death, upon the whole world.

In the midst of this, despite it all, the Son of God rules inwardly in the kingdom: 'The LORD said unto my Lord, Sit thou at my right hand, *until* I make thine enemies thy footstool.'

Meanwhile, from the ascension and throughout the age, 'the LORD shall send the rod of thy strength out of'–heavenly–'Zion'–from the glory of the Highest into the heart of his people here below–*'rule thou in the midst of thine enemies'*, Psalm 110:1,2.

But these conditions will not prevail for ever: only *'until'*. That is what Paul is saying.

Thus the people of God have been strangers, pilgrims, and sojourners through this present evil world from the beginning, looking for the resurrection and the world to come.

So it was with Abel, Enoch, Noah, Abraham, Sarah, and all the seed of promise until the coming and ministry of the Messiah. And thus it was in the beginning with the *ecclesia*, and of all the remnant separated from the subsequent apostasy.

Hence it is said 'know ye not that the friendship of the world is enmity with God? whosoever therefore will be a friend of the world is the enemy of God', James 4:4.

And no wonder, for, 'The kings of the earth set themselves, and the rulers take counsel together, against the LORD, and against his anointed, saying, Let us break their bands asunder, and cast away their cords from us. He that sitteth in the heavens shall laugh: the Lord shall have them in derision', Psalm 2:2-4.

Thus the heathen rage, and so the people imagine a vain thing, Psalm 2:1, for the truth is, above on high in the heavenly glory, 'the Lord God omnipotent reigneth', Revelation 19:6, and, even now, far over all, he saith, 'Yet have I set my king upon my holy hill of Zion', declaring the decree, 'Thou art my Son; this day have I begotten thee', Psalm 2:6,7.

Nevertheless in the heavens below, and in the darkness of this world beneath, the god of this world, called the 'devil', and Satan, blinds the minds of them that believe not, II Corinthians 4:4.

But, since the cross, the words have come to pass, 'Now is the judgment of this world: now shall the prince of this world be cast out'—that is, from the heavenly glory, to fall to the earth and heavens below—John 12:31, Revelation 12:9-17.

Moreover it is very clear that the Holy Ghost, abiding in the *ecclesia*, will convince the whole world of judgment, namely, of judgment upon this present age.

Why? Because the Spirit dwells in the saints, but he does not, and he will not, dwell in the world, as it is written of both the whole world, and of the prince that rules over it, 'of judgment, because the prince of this world is judged', John 16:11.

Then this present fallen world 'is not of the Father, but is of the world', I John 2:16, and over it and its kingdoms the 'devil' rules, as he saith, showing Jesus all the kingdoms of the world and the glory of them, 'All this power will I give thee, and the glory of them: for that is delivered unto me; and to whomsoever I will I give it', Matthew 4:8, Luke 4:6.

But, saith Christ to his own, 'If the world hate you, ye know that it hated me before it hated you. If ye were of the world,

51

the world would love his own: but because ye are not of the world, but I have chosen you out of the world, therefore the world hateth you', John 15:18,19.

Indeed, the Saviour 'gave himself for our sins, that he might deliver us from this present evil world, according to the will of God and our Father', Galatians 1:4.

Wherefore constantly we are employed in 'giving thanks unto the Father, which hath made us meet to be partakers of the inheritance of the saints in light: who hath delivered us from the power'—or authority—'of darkness, and hath translated us into the kingdom of his dear Son: in whom we have redemption through his blood, the forgiveness of sins', Colossians 1:12-14.

From all of which it is apparent that the whole world, begotten in the darkness and under the curse of the Fall, judged in itself and in its prince at the cross, is at enmity against God, and is the enemy of Christ.

If so, in that day, it shall fall beneath his feet. And so shall all his enemies, for, 'he must reign, till he hath put all enemies under his feet', I Corinthians 15:25.

'*All* enemies'? Who are these? Those over whom God hath raised him by the exceeding greatness of his power, according to the working of his mighty power, which he wrought in Christ when he raised him from the dead.

'And set him at his own right hand in the heavenly places, far above all principality, and power, and might, and dominion, and every name that is named, not only in this world, but also in that to come: and hath put all things under his feet', Ephesians 1:19-22.

As to us, inwardly in the kingdom of God, united with the King whom God hath set upon heavenly mount Zion, filled with the Spirit, but nevertheless still in this vile body and in the realm of this present evil world, consequently, 'we wrestle not against flesh and blood, but against principalities, against powers, against the rulers of the darkness of this world, against spiritual wickedness in heavenly places', Ephesians 6:12.

Here the enemies of Christ, whilst filling this present world, and encompassing it about – as 'the prince of the power of the air', Ephesians 2:2 – nevertheless ascend up from it in ranks of authority, even to 'heavenly places'.

This is the nature of 'this present evil world', Galatians 1:4, and indicates how vast, multiple, and varied are the spiritual and unseen enemies of Christ.

Nevertheless, high over all, in the heights of glory, he is seated on the throne of his Father, who 'must reign, till he hath put all' – mark that, *all* – 'enemies under his feet', I Corinthians 15:25.

Of all the books of the new testament, none opens so clearly or so vividly the ascension and reign of Christ in glory, and of his preserving the kingdom inwardly in his people below – despite this being in the midst of his enemies – nor of his final destruction of every one of those enemies, as does the Book of the Revelation.

However, these visions are couched in highly allegorical and figurative language, so that nothing is obvious and literal: everything is spiritual and mystical: nevertheless, for all this, *reality* is thus expressed.

Hence one may discern who are the enemies, how Christ brings them to judgment, and the manner of his bringing in the kingdom for God and the Father, world without end, Amen.

First appear the ecclesiastical enemies: more and more these fill and take over the outward profession of the *ecclesia*. But they will be judged, that judgment is pronounced, and destruction awaits them in the day of judgment. The meantime these hinder – by deceptive but fleshly duplication – and obscure the nature of the kingdom in this present evil age, in which they are so at home.

Next the Book of the Revelation depicts the worldly enemies of Christ and the people in whom he reigns, against whom the enmity and hatred of this world rages. But these shall be brought under, put down, and be judged in the day of his wrath.

Indeed, every one of the enemies – withal the affliction and tribulation caused by them to those of the kingdom of God throughout the age – shall be destroyed and brought into everlasting judgment and punishment at the coming of Christ to bring in the kingdom in glory, thus fulfilling the will, counsel and purpose of God and the Father.

However with the close of Revelation chapter 11, the lower, earthly sphere is left behind: an entirely new elevation, a heavenly realm of vastly higher altitude, filled with serried ranks of ever ascending spiritual powers, comes into view.

But if brought to view, it is only to show that these are already defeated, and if left in their positions and states of authority, it is only in the permissive will of God, and for no longer time than that concluded by the last day in which the King of kings and Lord of lords arises from the throne in the highest, to overthrow and judge these enemies for ever.

In that day he shall dissolve the heavens and the earth in flaming fire, melting the very elements, creating a new heavens and a new earth wherein dwelleth righteousness, bringing in the kingdom in the resurrection world without end, Amen.

In the allegorical figures of the Book of the Revelation the great red dragon, that old serpent, called the 'devil' and Satan, together with all his powers and ranks of authority in heavenly places, as the first beast, the second beast, the false prophet, not to mention Babylon the whore, and Babylon the city, are all cast alive into the lake that burneth with fire and brimstone, there to suffer the judgment of everlasting punishment.

Nor are these all, for, together with them – as if they were living embodiments – follow what is called 'the last enemy', together with his consort: 'And death and *hadēs* were cast into the lake of fire. This is the second death', Revelation 20:14.

But that is exactly what the apostle Paul taught – not under figurative language, but in the words of clear doctrine – to the *ecclesia* of God which was at Corinth concerning this same momentous truth.

'The last enemy that shall be destroyed is death', I Corinthians 15:26.

Now, since death is that which occurs to *the body* – and cannot refer to the soul – then by what else shall the last enemy be destroyed than by the resurrection from the dead?

And this, in the creation, will, counsel, and purpose of God, is precisely what the apostle declares in I Corinthians 15:20-28 concerning the consummation of all things.

To achieve such a tremendous climax to the ages, to all time, to this present world, to every enemy, all things had been put in subjection beneath the feet of the Son of God in the ascension.

Nothing and no one – save he who committed all things to the Son, putting all things under him – I say, nothing either lives or has existence that Almighty God, even his Father, the Highest, has not put into subjection under him, that he might subdue all things unto himself.

That is, that he might subdue every enemy, bring this present evil age to a conclusion, command the fiery deluge, raise the very dead, create a new heavens and a new earth, bring in the world to come whereof we speak, and, finally, deliver up the kingdom to God and the Father.

So teaches the apostle: 'For he hath put all things under his feet. But when he saith all things are put under him, it is manifest that he is excepted, which did put all things under him', I Corinthians 15:27.

'And when all things shall be subdued unto him, then shall the Son also himself be subject unto him that put all things under him, that God may be all in all', I Corinthians 15:28.

The words 'And *when* all things shall be subdued unto him' are indicative of the end of the period commencing with the ascension and concluding with the descent of the Son at his second coming to judgment.

Then all things shall have been, and will be, subdued unto him.

This period began with the fulfilment of the prophecy, 'Sit thou at my right hand', and will finish with the consummation of the text '*until* I make thine enemies thy footstool', Psalm 110:1.

Of this Peter speaks on the day of Pentecost: 'Therefore being by the right hand of God exalted, and having received of the Father the promise of the Holy Ghost, he hath shed forth this, which ye now see and hear. For David is not ascended into the heavens: but he saith himself, The LORD said unto my Lord, Sit thou on my right hand, until I make thy foes thy footstool.

'Therefore let all the house of Israel know assuredly, that God hath made that same Jesus, whom ye have crucified, both Lord and Christ', Acts 2:33-36.

And so expounds the writer to the Hebrews, saying, 'Thou crownedst him with glory and honour, and didst set him over the works of thy hands: thou hast put all things in subjection under his feet. For in that he put all in subjection under him, he left nothing that is not put under him.'

But, if so, Why are all things as they are? Because there is a *period*, an *age*, between his being exalted, and his bringing his almighty power to bear upon his enemies:

'But now we see not *yet* all things put under him. But we see Jesus, who was made a little lower than the angels for the suffering of death, crowned with glory and honour', Hebrews 2:7-9.

During this his reign from the heights of glory *'until'*– at the last – he rises to put all things, vanquished, in subjection under himself at the last day, his authority is yet absolute: *even now* the *Father* hath put *all things* under his feet.

And so it must be, until he rises up in wrath and vengeance to make his enemies – *all* his enemies – his footstool for ever.

Still, even until that day, he reigns in glory in perfect patience, knowing, declaring, '*All things are delivered unto me of my Father*', Matthew 11:27, and, '*All* authority is given unto me *in heaven and in earth*', Matthew 28:18.

And, again, he saith unto the Father of himself, 'thou hast given him authority over all flesh', John 17:2.

Likewise the apostle teaches, 'he raised him from the dead, and set him at his own right hand in the heavenly places, *far above* all principality, and power, and might, and dominion, and every name that is named, not only in this world, but also in that which is to come:

'And *hath put all things under his feet*, and gave him to be the head *over all things* to the *ecclesia*, which is his body, the fulness of him that filleth all in all', Ephesians 1:20-23.

Hence, 'he hath put all things under his feet. But when he saith all things are put under him, it is manifest that he is excepted, which did put all things under him.

'And *when* all things shall be *subdued*' – not *put* only, but *subdued* actually, in the day of his wrath and vengeance – 'then shall the Son also himself be subject unto him that put all things under him, that God may be all in all', I Corinthians 15:27,28.

This answers to Revelation chapters 21 and 22; all the enemies destroyed, time being no more, the world to come having come to pass, the kingdom delivered up to the Father, the Son also himself being subject unto him that put all things under him, that God may be all in all.

The Son also himself? Subject? What is this? It is the Son *in terms of his humanity, the Son considered as head of the body, namely*, of that sonship in manhood which is conformed to his own image.

Head of the body, he is one with that body, in manhood after himself. New manhood: that *is* sonship, 'for we are members of his body, of his flesh, and of his bones'.

Just as Eve, taken out of the side of Adam, was of his flesh, and of his bones. This is a great mystery: but I speak concerning Christ and the *ecclesia*, Ephesians 5:30-32.

This signifies the second man, the last Adam, the quickening Spirit, one with his brethren, all alike in new manhood, he glorified in them, and they in him. In figure, thus was Adam glorified in Eve. But in Christ the reality transcends the figure higher than the heavens transcend the earth.

For it shall come to pass in truth that Christ shall glorify God in that unique risen manhood of sonship which at once declares him to be one with his brethren and one in and with the Father and with the Spirit.

Thus God shall be all in all, and seen to be all in all, filling the unity of that peerless humanity which stands for evermore in the oneness of sonship in Christ.

In manhood one with his own, in deity one with the Father and with the Spirit. Filled with the fulness of God.

All in all; Father, Son, and Holy Ghost, glorified to everlasting in the Son and his bride, of his body: flesh of his flesh, and bone of his bone. And if so, in the resurrection from the dead.

And, these things being given – and they *are* given – in heaven or in earth, in time or in eternity, in deity or in humanity, in life or in death, in this world or in the next, in counsel or in purpose, in the first creation or in the last: How, how, 'how say some among you that there is no resurrection of the dead?', I Corinthians 15:12.

Fifth; the assurance of the resurrection the motive for the baptism of those who confront death; stand in jeopardy; die daily; and face martyrdom, putting the Corinthians to shame, I Corinthians 15:29-34.

In this passage the apostle passes from 'they' to 'we' to 'I', all providing examples brought to bear on 'you'–the Corinthians– so as to shame them by these exemplary instances of the faith of God's elect, who show forth so evidently what it is to follow in the steps of Jesus, denying themselves, taking up their cross daily:

'For whosoever will save his life shall lose it; but whosoever shall lose his life for my sake and for the gospel's, the same shall save it', Mark 8:35.

Then what is this denying of the truth of the resurrection of the dead–essential and integral to the evangel–on the part of the Corinthians?

59

'Know ye not, that so many of us as were baptized into Jesus Christ were baptized into his death?', Romans 6:3.

'Now if we be dead with Christ, we believe that we shall also live with him', Romans 6:8.

This is the essence of the context of this entire passage, and of each example brought forward to enforce it, whether it were the 'they' – verse 29 – the 'we' – verse 30 – or the 'I' – verses 31 and 32.

'Else what shall *they* do' – whoever *they* are, they were not conspicuous amongst *you*, the Corinthians! – 'which are baptized for the dead, if the dead rise not at all?'

If the dead rise not at all, then they who are baptized, were baptized for nothing: in which case what should their poor deluded lost souls do?

But they are *not* poor deluded lost souls: they are baptized into Christ's death indeed, nor shall they be disappointed in the issue. Were they to be, and the evangel – God forbid! – found to be untrue, 'Why are they then baptized for the dead?'.

Why? Because the evangel *is* true; because they *were* 'buried with him by baptism into death'; and because 'Now is Christ risen from the dead, and become the firstfruits of them that slept'.

Then, O ye Corinthians, *follow their example*, instead of *condoning those among you who denied it*, I Corinthians 15:29.

Surely it ought to be superfluous to state the obvious – if only from the context, let alone the absurdity – that 'Else what shall they do which are baptized for the dead?', I Corinthians 15:29, *cannot* refer to living persons being baptized on behalf of others who had died.

I feel no need to point out the use of the preposition ὑπὲρ in connection with the genitive plural of νεκρός, telling as is this usage when coupled with τῶν νεκρῶν, supporting the correct interpretation in context.

But why not? Because it is unnecessary to state the obvious, let alone buttress that statement with the niceties of Greek grammar.

The passage *must* refer to *oneself* being reckoned dead. 'He that believeth and is baptized shall be saved', Mark 16:16, can hardly refer to anything other than living believers being baptized for themselves. Nevertheless the figure of baptism shows that it was in view of their being dead.

Again, Jesus, commanding the eleven to teach all nations, baptizing them, scarcely supposes their going forth with spades, exhuming decomposed corpses, first reciting doctrine into the air over what was left of them, then, having soaked the grisly remains with water, returning the sodden corpses to the grave.

How much less can Jesus' commandment mean that each of the eleven was to go through the charade of doing the same thing one to another over the grave as if one of them could stand in for the buried corpse beneath their feet.

What! The holy apostles performing so ridiculous a ritual?

Yet, in effect, this is the monstrous perversity invented from I Corinthians 15:29 by those blasphemous heretics called 'Mormons', a deluded sect led to destruction by the insane ramblings of Joseph Smith.

And *these*, with *their* record, dare to call themselves 'The Church of Jesus Christ of Latter Day Saints'?

Such a synagogue of Satan may spruce up the outward man by a form of the law slyly incorporated into their appallingly sacrilegious fantasy called the 'Book of Mormon', hiding the blasphemies *really* held behind a chameleon-like appearance, but the discerning and spiritual know who gave them the 'kingdom' and 'glory of them' represented by their Salt Lake City prosperity.

Hence I repeat: the words 'What shall they do which are baptized for the dead?', neither wrench the larger context of I Corinthians chapter 15 nor the local context of verses 29-34, nor do they give the faintest warrant to those who reduce the passage to a perverse absurdity.

This is in fact a text wholly consistent with the teaching on baptism throughout the new testament.

It is unthinkable that the words 'They which are baptized for the dead' could refer to one being baptized for another who had died already. It *must* point to *oneself* being dead.

That is what one is baptized for: to show forth by that ordinance the being reckoned – and reckoning oneself – dead with Christ *already*.

Indeed, more: the being reckoned dead with Christ *when he died*. That is, before one's own decease *in practice*, so that *his* death is accounted of God *as one's own* even prior to what is called in scripture 'falling on sleep'.

And if so, this is equally true of his rising from the dead: 'For if' – by baptism – 'we have been planted together' – with him, in death – 'in the likeness of his death, *we shall be also in the likeness of his resurrection*', Romans 6:5.

If those who are thus baptized are not so raised, then everything will have proved to have been in vain: 'Else what shall they do which are baptized for the dead, if the dead rise not at all? why are they then baptized for the dead?', I Corinthians 15:29.

Why? Because just as their faith declared that by baptism they were dead and buried with Christ *already*, so the same faith showed that by rising up out of baptism they should arise from the dead at his coming: 'Christ the firstfruits; afterward they that are Christ's at his coming', I Corinthians 15:23.

'But now *is* Christ risen from the dead, and become the first-fruits of them that slept', I Corinthians 15:20.

That is what they shall do which are baptized for the dead, because the dead must *surely* rise after all; thus *that* is why they are baptized for the dead, because *after it* they shall rise again at the coming of the Lord for his own.

Evidently therefore those who are baptized for the dead are so baptized for two reasons.

One, their baptism *shows their present death and burial in the sight of God and in the inward witness of the Spirit*: 'Know ye not, that so many of us as were baptized into Jesus Christ were baptized *into his death*? Therefore we are buried with him by baptism *into death*', Romans 6:3,4.

Then, we are seen as *dead with him*, and, indeed, this is how we see ourselves: 'Likewise reckon ye also yourselves to be dead indeed unto sin, but alive unto God through Jesus Christ our Lord', Romans 6:11.

'Buried with him in baptism, wherein also ye are risen with him through the faith of the operation of God, who hath raised him from the dead', Colossians 2:12.

The second reason why those who are baptized for the dead are so baptized follows: it is in view of the death of *their own bodies*, when they fall asleep in Christ.

They believe that their death *does not count*. Why not? *Because it has already been counted.*

When? When they were baptized for the dead.

'Jesus said unto her, I am the resurrection, and the life: he that believeth in me, *though he were dead*, yet shall he live: and whosoever liveth and believeth in me *shall never die*. Believest thou this?', John 11:25,26.

We certainly do believe it, and so do they.

They? Who? Why, 'they', all of them, who are baptized for the dead. That was, and is, the reason for their being so baptized, *because* such a baptism *shows openly* what they believe.

The difficulty in I Corinthians 15:29 comes from the word 'for', as in 'baptized *for* the dead'. There is no English equivalent.

In fact, the Greek ὑπὲρ has virtually been transliterated into the English by the word 'hyper'. And what will you make of that?

In geometry, if one considers a cube, ὑπὲρ, *over*, would apply to the upper plane. But then one must consider in grammar whether it is with the accusative or genitive. And what will you make of that?

Not much, whoever you are: and the worst you can be is an academic know-all. The best, one who knows nothing save that Christ is our wisdom, and that the Spirit is truth.

Take the text as it stands and one *naturally* reads it the wrong way. But it is *essential* not to do so. Rather, one must guage the nuance of the word 'for'–the nearest the translators could get to ὑπὲρ in this instance–from the context of both verse and passage.

Not to mention comparing both with *every other place* in which 'baptized' and 'baptism' occur.

Such places will always be consistent with each other. As God cannot deny himself, neither can scripture deny itself.

So then, they which are baptized for the dead are baptized *now* for when they are dead *afterwards*. Why? Because all their hope lies in the resurrection.

'If in this life only we have hope in Christ, we are of all men most miserable', verse 19.

But *now* we – and they – reckon ourselves dead, that is, to have died, so that *when* our bodies die in fact, all we can see is *resurrection*: '*Else* what shall they do which are baptized for the dead, *if the dead rise not at all*? why are they *then* baptized for the dead?' Indeed, Why are they baptized at all?

In such a case they are baptized for nothing but a delusion! And not them only, but all of us. And not us only, but all who have fallen asleep in Christ before us: 'Then they also which are fallen asleep in Christ are perished', verse 18.

But they *hoped* not to perish. That was why they showed their faith and hope when they were baptized.

They were baptized for the dead, not for the perishing. 'Else what shall they do which are baptized for the dead, if the dead rise not at all? why are they then baptized for the dead?'

They – and we – were and are baptized by faith *now* for *when* they – and we – were and will be dead in fact.

They themselves – or we ourselves – were baptized 'for' *their own death, that it should be made manifest beforehand that they had died, and were dead, in and with Christ*. They are 'passed from death unto life', John 5:24, and shall neither see nor taste of death, John 8:51,52. Hence note that verse 29 is a question.

In fact it is *two* questions. And hypothetical questions at that. And *both* have death and resurrection in view.

Question *that*, and *then* where are they? Or we?

In truth, then they, or we, are perished. However, in reality, there *is* no question. Such questions are merely hypothetical and rhetorical. Not real at all. It is the *resurrection* that is real. And *that* is why they—and we—were baptized for the dead.

Baptized for the dead? But it was—and is—not *just* death that was—and is—in view. It is death *and resurrection*. But, evidently, one must die and join the dead before being raised. Then, one is baptized 'for the dead'.

The dead? Which dead? The dead as such. Then, being baptized, it is as if at the time one were standing over and above them that are buried, baptism being an acknowledgement not just that one will join them in their graves, but that in doing so it will be as *having died with Christ already*.

And Christ is 'the resurrection and the life'. Then, baptized for the dead? Yes, but as well call it 'death'. It is the being baptized with a view to death: to joining the dead, over which now one lives. But only till the grave claims our mortality.

So one is baptized by faith in Christ to show that one is baptized *facing one's dying and joining the dead*. Yes, baptized for the dead. But not with a view to *staying* dead: with a view to *rising from the dead*.

That is what one is declaring—*they* are declaring—by faith, and that is what Paul means by this difficult expression.

From which it follows that the reader is advised to read 'the dead'—as in 'baptized for the dead'—in terms of 'for when one is dead oneself'; for when one leaves the land of the living and joins 'the dead' in a collective sense.

That is it: 'for the dead' collectively. The word must be read as describing all those who have passed into the domain of death.

'The dead', I Corinthians 15:29, refers to *that state as such*, rather than one's own individual passage into it. 'The dead' in this verse is indicative of a certain realm – the realm of death – not one's actual decease and individual entrance into that realm.

It is the condition itself, not the individuals who have passed into it. One is baptized not for *them*, but for *it*.

It? Yes, the dominion under which all the dead lie, the domain into which every one of the deceased has passed. A state, that is, into which at the last *they* must pass – I Corinthians 15:29 – and *we* must pass. However, both *they* and *we* were and are baptized because we have confronted *it* before it confronts *us*.

And in that confrontation we have taken the shield of faith, believing that *already* we have died with Christ, and being assured that just as he who died for us rose again, so also we shall be partakers of his resurrection.

That is why they, and we, are 'baptized for the dead', I Corinthians 15:29.

By certain examples from his own continual experience, and that of others who suffered even unto death, or were suffering with the expectation of dying for the testimony which they held, the apostle shows how the faithful were to live: in the shadow of death, but in the hope of the resurrection.

'And why stand we in jeopardy every hour? I protest by your rejoicing which I have in Christ Jesus our Lord, I die daily.

'If after the manner of men I have fought with beasts at Ephesus, what advantageth it me, if the dead rise not? let us eat and drink; for tomorrow we die', I Corinthians 15:30-32.

Paul, and all the brethren with him, stood in jeopardy every hour. He was persecuted, men sought his destruction daily, false brethren went behind his back no sooner had they heard of yet another work being raised up under his ministry, or else some other person having been converted by his gospel.

So these fruitless, useless, worthless false brethren could not leave him alone, consumed with envy and fury, pursuing him as soon as he had departed, at his heels wherever he went, and in whatever country, stirring up the authorities also, even unto Caesar himself.

This was jeopardy indeed; here was persecution – according to the testimony of Jesus – of a truth.

And so it is with those sent of Christ, filled with the Spirit, running in the steps of the apostle, having received the same evangel, being blessed with like fruitfulness, even unto this day.

These also the false brethren hate, persecute, put out of the synagogue, and pursue with relentless energy.

As their fathers did to the psalmist, so these also heap iniquity upon the head of the servants of God, bearing false witness, purveying lies and evil tales which they and their sort invent and multiply from that day to this.

And who were these that so persecuted the servants of God, filled with the Spirit of Christ? Oh, they were the chief priests, elders, doctors of the law, rulers, scribes, Pharisees, Sadducees, and their hosts of followers after the flesh in Israel. But not in the Israel of God. These carry no weight there.

And so it is with their children even unto this present time in their 'churches' as they call them, with their 'evangelicalism' as they call it, persecuting the servants of God as their fathers before them persecuted Paul; the ministers of Christ; the psalmist; and, indeed, *all* the prophets and *every one* of the faithful in the land.

It does not worry these people that *they* are not persecuted.

No; supine and oblivious in self-righteousness, complacency, and pride, if one should point out that whereas *all* the godly were *always* persecuted, but that they are *never* persecuted, they would raise supercilious eyebrows and retire from such a madman as soon as decently possible.

Persecution? Foolish nonsense: What? *them* persecuted? with *their* 'Christ-like' spirit? with all the good *they* do in and to the world? Don't be ridiculous: Who would want to persecute *them*?

As to that so-called Servant of the Lord, and the people with him—not that there are many left; most we have managed to turn back—indeed, one expects they have all gone by now, leaving this wicked and deluded 'Servant' to his own devices: well, *he* ought to be persecuted, certainly.

He *should* stand in jeopardy every hour, besides any that are foolish enough to be with him, what with the volume of mis-information we have quite rightly spread abroad into all the earth beforehand, at present, after the event, and always behind the back.

Thus by the slander, lies, libel, and malicious gossip dissemin-ated and recycled by these 'evangelicals' and their 'churches', all to stop Christ speaking by the mouth of his Servant, and to prejudice beforehand any would-be hearers or readers, they hope to have done God service, John 15:18,19; 16:1-3.

Hence like their father the devil, the father of lies, John 8:43-45, these set to with a will, showing themselves the children of the accuser of the brethren with a witness.

Wherefore, these who are *not* persecuted, *do* persecute. But we who *are* persecuted, do *not* persecute.

By this sure mark you can tell the difference. For as a sheep before his shearers is dumb, so we open not our mouths, going as a lamb to the slaughter, while these howl for our reputations, life, and, could they, even our blood, for all they are worth.

And that is all that they *are* worth. If not, 'why stand we in jeopardy every hour?', I Corinthians 15:30.

But we suffer it silently, because we look for a better resurrection. Then let the Corinthians–and all others–go and do likewise.

'I die daily', cried Paul, the Servant of Christ, I Corinthians 15:31. Yes, he died *daily*. Well, he expected that: it was why he had been baptized for the dead.

'Are they ministers of Christ? (I speak as a fool) I am more; in labours more abundant, in stripes above measure, in prisons more frequent, in deaths oft.

'Of the Jews five times received I forty stripes save one. Thrice was I beaten with rods, once was I stoned, thrice I suffered shipwreck, a night and a day I have been in the deep; in journeyings often,

'In perils of waters, in perils of robbers, in perils by mine own countrymen, in perils by the heathen, in perils in the city, in perils in the wilderness, in perils in the sea, in perils among false brethren;

'In weariness and painfulness, in watchings often, in hunger and thirst, in fastings often, in cold and nakedness.

'Besides those things that are without, that which cometh upon me daily, the care of all the churches. Who is weak, and I am not weak? who is offended, and I burn not? If I must needs glory, I will glory of the things which concern mine infirmities.

'The God and Father of our Lord Jesus Christ, which is blessed for evermore, knoweth that I lie not.

'In Damascus the governor under Aretus the king kept the city of the Damascenes with a garrison, desirous to apprehend me: and through a window in a basket was I let down by the wall, and escaped his hands', II Corinthians 11:23-33.

O, Paul died daily. 'I protest by your rejoicing which I have in Christ Jesus our Lord, I die daily', I Corinthians 15:31.

'If after the manner of men I have fought with beasts at Ephesus, what advantageth it me, if the dead rise not? let us eat and drink; for tomorrow we die', I Corinthians 15:32.

There are no grounds for supposing that this analogy of Paul has anything to do with the uprising recorded in Acts 19:23-41.

Although the enmity of the silversmiths directed against the apostle by Demetrius of Ephesus began with a gathering of those of like trade addressed by him, the subsequent uproar that spread like wildfire to the confusion of the whole city was caused by the cry 'Great is Diana of the Ephesians', Acts 19:28, as though *this* notion were in jeopardy. By then, Paul was forgotten.

Indeed it was the two Macedonians, Gaius and Aristarchus, who were caught and rushed into the theatre, forthwith filled with crowds in a state of sheer confusion, conflicting in their opinion of why they were there at all:

'Some therefore cried one thing, and some another: for the assembly was confused; and the more part knew not wherefore they were come together', Acts 19:32.

Now it was the turn of Gaius and Aristarchus to be forgotten, for out of the mêlée they drew forth one Alexander, the Jews— of all people—putting him forth in the midst of the multitude. 'And Alexander beckoned with the hand, and would have made his defence unto the people.

'But when they knew that he was a Jew'—a Jew, mark; not a Christian: Demetrius' cause had been lost in the turmoil—'*a Jew*, all with one voice about the space of two hours cried out, Great is Diana of the Ephesians', Acts 19:34.

But what had that to do with the apostle Paul, who, by now, was far distant, and, in any event, never entered into the theatre? How can *this* be his 'fighting with beasts at Ephesus', as if Acts 19:23-41 were anything whatsoever to do with I Corinthians 15:32?

Note that Paul speaks in the first person: 'If after the manner of men *I* have fought': but he was not there on that occasion, and, if not, how could he have fought with beasts or anything else?

Again, those who *were* there—either the disappearing Gaius and Aristarchus or the gesturing Alexander—were at no stage remotely engaged in fighting: at the very most, they were no more than verbally on the defensive.

Furthermore it was the multitude that occupied the theatre: by the remotest stretch of the imagination not even the rudest and most ignorant of commentators could call that audience 'beasts'.

Finally, if ever man and beast *did* come together in such a place, it would be in the *arena*, not in the tiered seating of the theatre itself. It was the *latter* which would have been filled with and occupied by the *spectators*.

However in Acts 19 *Alexander*—certainly not Paul—*was* in the arena—by himself—seeking for two hours to make his defence before the audience of *men*, during not one single moment of which was the solitary occupant fighting against any wild animal, much less a plurality of beasts.

Besides all this—in any event—what have any of these affairs to do with the absent Paul, who, incidentally, writes in the *first person* in his analogy in I Corinthians 15:32?

These affairs had nothing at all to do with him, neither had the theatre when on that occasion it was so used.

Riots were not the purpose of the renowned theatre: *entertainment* was. Or, at least, what the people thought of as entertainment.

In which case gladiatorial combat, or men called out and chosen to fight against wild beasts, were the choice attractions. And it is to the latter of these that Paul alludes in his analogy.

But if so, how *did* men fight with beasts at Ephesus? By constraint. It was required of them: they were forced into it: the crowd loved it.

Failed or unpopular gladiators, persons fallen from grace with the authorities, recaptured runaway slaves, insubordinate soldiers, prisoners, condemned persons–any of these–perforce were armed, perhaps given a shield, and were condemned to enter the arena in the sight of the caged wild beasts under the high surrounding peripheral walls.

At a signal, the cage doors were drawn up, and the mortal combat began. Such rejected, disgraced, or condemned men were those who thus fought with beasts at Ephesus, who *must* do so, and would almost certainly be mauled to death in the event.

Knowing this, what was their language beforehand? 'Let us eat and drink; for tomorrow we die', I Corinthians 15:32.

But this, though language after the manner of men, was not the language of *every one* of those forcibly exposed to such slaughter. In the persecutions which had raged against the Christians, and would yet rage again, those who refused to deny Christ, or compromise the faith, faced the same death.

But with an entirely different attitude; with a wholly contrary utterance; and with an altogether distinct motive and prospect.

73

Nor did they fight, however vainly those fought—after the manner of men—who had eaten and drunken the night before. But these praised and prayed the night through.

They went defenceless to the same slaughter, carried mortally wounded and flailing in agony in the slavering jaws and beneath the lacerating claws of the beasts sent to execute so bloody and cruel a death upon them, to the delight of the multitude.

Whereas those that put up a fight braved it out the day before—'Let us eat and drink; for tomorrow we die'—these, as sheep delivered to the slaughter, opened not their mouths, unless it were in the singing of psalms, hymns, and spiritual songs, or the repetition of memorized scriptures.

Whence such fortitude? How come such an absolute contrast between the two classes facing the same death?

Because the one with reckless abandon laughed at death. But the other with faith in Christ believed in the resurrection of the dead.

Were not the resurrection the motive, their conduct would have been inexplicable.

Why be martyred? Why suffer? Why not compromise? Because 'if in this life only we have hope in Christ, we are of all men most miserable.' Hence they loved not their lives unto the death.

Why be thrown to the lions unless, after death, they believed that 'in Christ shall all be made alive'?

Likewise 'others were tortured, not accepting deliverance; that they might obtain a better resurrection: and others had trial of cruel mockings and scourgings, yea, moreover of bonds and imprisonment: they were stoned, they were sawn asunder, were tempted, were slain with the sword:

'They wandered about in sheepskins and goatskins; being destitute, afflicted, tormented; (of whom the world was not worthy:) they wandered in deserts, and in mountains, and in dens and caves of the earth', Hebrews 11:35-38.

Yes, and before Paul wrote, and after it, his constant expectation was to be a partaker of the same martyrdom—or one much like to it—so that hypothetically and in an analogy he could declare to the Corinthians concerning the stupendous prospect of the resurrection of the dead, 'If after the manner of men'—were it so: to die like them; yet so unlike them—'I have fought with beasts at Ephesus, what advantageth it me, if the dead rise not?'

Why die for faith in Christ, if he rose not, and the dead rise not?

Or, if one *must* die, why not speak beforehand as did the reckless—'let us eat and drink; for tomorrow we die'?

Why not? Because after death, we who have died with Christ, shall also live with him: 'for since by man came death, by man came also the resurrection of the dead', I Corinthians 15:21.

Now, who will the Corinthians follow? To the speech of which shall they listen? Let them beware of those to whom they gave ear, lest worldly wisdom or heathen recklessness corrupt their faith in Christ.

'Be not deceived: evil communications'—such as *'let us eat and drink, for tomorrow we die'*, taunted in self-mockery by rash and lawless men—'evil communications corrupt good manners', I Corinthians 15:33.

'Awake to righteousness': keep yourselves pure, clean, holy, separate; shun worldliness, worldly talk, worldly company: *keep the resurrection from the dead in constant view.*

'Awake to righteousness, and sin not'; as you have sinned, denying the resurrection, or suffering those who do so, mingling their words with the words of God to which you should have been wholly given: *sin not!*

'For some have not the knowledge of God': else they would never have been reduced to such shameful corruption from the way of life and the truth of the evangel. 'I speak this to your shame', I Corinthians 15:34.

SIXTH; THE FOLLY OF QUESTIONING THE RESURRECTION OF THE DEAD SHOWN FROM CREATION; BY REVELATION; AND THROUGH THE OPENING OF A MYSTERY, I CORINTHIANS 15:35-58.

Because the folly of questioning the resurrection of the dead springs from the lawless rationalizing of intellectual presumption, the apostle anticipates the questionings which necessarily follow from 'some among you' who say 'that there is no resurrection of the dead'.

He expected this of such persons, despite all that he had taught up to this point, knowing full well the intractable nature of such arrogant rationalists and would-be intellectuals, who, exalting themselves above the most High, in effect at once argue the Creator out of the creation, and scoff at the very thought of his creating *anything further not yet in existence.*

Paul sets about deflating such swollen arrogance, piercing through its bloated conceit with the sword of the Spirit, which is the word of God.

He is determined to subdue such limiting of the Almighty to the confines of the carnal mind; to the boundaries of the things which can be seen; and to the imposition of precedents set by natural laws.

He goes to war against every form of intellectual rebellion, but not with fleshly weapons. For he did not war after the flesh. The weapons of his warfare were not carnal, but mighty through God to the pulling down of the strongholds of science falsely so-called, casting down reasonings, and bringing into captivity every thought to the obedience of Christ.

'But some one will say, How are the dead raised up? and with what body do they come?', I Corinthians 15:35.

If eye hath not seen, nor ear heard, neither hath it entered into the heart of man the things which God hath prepared for them that love him, I Corinthians 2:9, what kind of fool occupies himself with peering into the invisible; listening for the inaudible; and reasoning about the incomprehensible?

If such things lie beyond the senses, stretch past the imagination, exceed all known dimensions, confound every perceivable precedent, transcend all human understanding, and surpass anything ever dreamed of since man had existence, I repeat, What kind of fool goes about posing questions concerning superlative mysteries which lie altogether beyond this present world and visible creation?

Stupid questions! They are never answered. They cannot be answered.

How can anybody know what has never been envisaged? How can anyone comprehend what has not yet taken place? How can anything be explained that lies beyond human capacity to grasp?

The truth is, had these audacious questioners mortified their carnal minds and natural reasonings to submit to the confines of faith in the evangel, such folly would never have entered into their heads, much less passed through their lips.

But the fact that Paul anticipates such utterances shows to what depths of shame even some among the Corinthians could debase and drag down that evangel which once so earnestly they professed. What folly! 'Thou fool.'

Yet, nevertheless, bearing all things, believing all things, hoping all things, enduring all things, kindly condescending to lift up the fool out of his folly, the apostle brings that to bear upon him, which will greatly assist in his recovery, by causing him to see things on earth, in heaven, by revelation, and through a mystery, which are calculated at once to bring back to repentance and forward into faith.

First, things on earth, and things in heaven; that is, from creation: the apostle seems to bring forth three, but on examination in fact it must be four examples either of *change* or of *difference*.

The first example is that of seed that is sown; the second that of different kinds of flesh; thirdly, Paul points out the distinction in glory between heavenly and earthly bodies; finally, confining himself to the heavens, he points to the varying glories of the sun, moon, and the stars.

All these he cites as examples in the will, counsel, and power of God to cause changes and create differences in glory from a creation *already in existence*. Then why not of a creation *yet to come*?

In quoting verses 36-41 I use the interlinear translation from 'The Englishman's Greek New Testament', published by Samuel Bagster in 1877, this giving a very clear idea of the Greek, which, laid side by side with the Authorized, will prove helpful to the elucidation of the original.

'Fool; what thou sowest is not quickened unless it die. And what thou sowest, not the body that shall be thou sowest, but a bare grain, it may be of wheat, or of some one of the rest; and God to it gives a body according as he willed, and to each of the seeds its own body.

'Not every flesh is the same flesh, but one flesh of men, and another of beasts, and another of fishes, and another of birds.

'And bodies heavenly, and bodies earthly: but different is the glory of the heavenly, and different that of the earthly.

'One glory of the sun, and another glory of the moon, and another of the stars; star differing from star in glory', I Corinthians 15:36-41.

The first example in creation which hints at the resurrection is the longest, and certainly the most telling. It concerns not only *difference* but difference through *change*. Moreover, not only change, but a change *of the original thing*. Furthermore, a change of the original thing *effected through life from the dead*.

Now, this exemplifies the resurrection. And it does so in the present creation, year in and year out, before our very eyes. And what kind of a fool is he that ignores this staggering evidence? Answer: A blind fool.

Now, a sower sows the bare grain. He ploughs, scatters, harrows, so that the seed falls into the ground, and dies: 'Except a corn of wheat fall into the ground *and die*, it abideth alone', John 12:24. It abideth alone; that is, it retaineth its present state. *But that is not its destiny.*

Its destiny is to *die*. It was not brought forth to exist without change. It was not formed to abide in this present state. It was formed to fall into the ground and die.

And, dead, to be covered over by the earth, buried and left alone. By man. But not by God. Though dead, it shall—it must—rise again. But not in the same state: 'And that which thou sowest, thou *sowest not that body that shall be*.'

For a season, what was sown lay buried under the earth, but at the last, at the appointed time, out of the earth, up from the seed that died, rising again, a green blade, a shoot, a stalk, then the full ear.

But that was not what was sown.

No; for what was sown was *long ago* dead and buried. But what is risen is at last *that life – yea, that body – which must and shall rise from the dead.*

But it is *not the body which was sown*. It is *the body which rises from the dead*. For 'God giveth it'– in the resurrection from the dead –'a body as it hath pleased him, and to every seed his own body', I Corinthians 15:38.

Again, 'All flesh is not the same flesh: but one kind of flesh is of men, and another flesh of beasts, another of fishes, and another of birds', verse 39. Yes, Paul, but what has *that* to do with the resurrection?

This is the apostle's second example, and it is given to illustrate *how differently God could, God did, and therefore God can, create utterly distinct kinds of living substances, each suited to its proper order.*

The flesh of man to rule over all; the flesh of beasts to graze in the field; the flesh of fishes to swim in the sea; and the flesh of birds to fly in the air.

Yes, but although flesh as such is common to each of the four, so diverse is the one from the other, each suited to its own kind of life and proper realm, formed each after its kind to multiply variously throughout the world for the duration of this present age, the whole combining to testify beyond all reasonable doubt that the Lord God not only *can* but *will* create that which is suited to the body of glory and immortality raised from the dead in the everlasting kingdom that pertains to the world to come.

And how much more is that *new* creation certain, considering– for all its wonderful diversity– the futility into which this present world has fallen, to groan and travail under pain, corruption, and death, so long as time shall last?

Who in their right mind can suppose that the Creator will rest with *that* state of affairs?

Only a fool could make such a supposition.

And only a fool could presume that he who made such suited diversity of flesh in *this* world, cannot again exert the same power in the last day suitably to clothe the body of resurrection in the world that is to come.

Thirdly, Paul compares heavenly bodies and earthly bodies; or, as the Authorized will have it, bodies celestial with bodies terrestrial. 'And bodies heavenly, and bodies earthly: but different is the glory of the heavenly, and different that of the earthly', I Corinthians 15:40.

Here are realms as different as time and eternity, with a glory peculiar to each, one that of the heavenly, the other that of the earthly. If so, why should not the Creator reserve a present glory for time, and a coming glory for eternity? For even now this suggests one glory, which passes, for this world; and another glory, which abides, for the world to come.

If there is a glory to the bodies that exist in the world, and this shines forth to show God's eternal power and Godhead in the things that are made upon the face of the earth, how diversely does that same power and Godhead appear in the creation of the things above in the heavens?

With what a distinct luminosity appears also the glory of the heavenly bodies, whether shining by day or by night? Compare the two, bodies terrestrial and bodies celestial, and what can one conclude?

The glory of God seen in the things which he has created and made is so wonderfully evident, yet so utterly different, that the heaven and the earth combine to declare and make manifest throughout time the new heavens and the new earth yet to come throughout everlasting glory.

Likewise, if the respective glory is so distinct from all that exists – whether terrestrial or celestial – in a world and age that is doomed to pass away, how much more glorious must be all that pertains to the new heavens and the new earth in an eternity which shall never pass away?

For it follows by a law of progression that just as there is a comparative glory between bodies heavenly and earthly in this age, there must also be one glory that pertains to the present creation, and another glory that pertains to that which is to come.

And if all this be true of heavenly and earthly bodies, whether in this world or the next, it most certainly must be true of the bodies of the saints in the resurrection of the dead.

Which is what Paul had set out to demonstrate in this third example of the things that differ, visible before the eyes of men, yet indicative of the resurrection yet to come, I Corinthians 15:40.

'There is one glory of the sun, and another glory of the moon, and another glory of the stars: for one star differeth from another star in glory', I Corinthians 15:41.

Here is the fourth and last example from creation given by the apostle Paul to lead the reflective mind to the witness of the Creator to the resurrection of the dead.

At first this might appear to be a continuation of the previous verse; however, but a moment's consideration shows that it cannot be so.

In the third example, verse 40, the apostle distinguishes between the glory of celestial – or heavenly – bodies and the glory of terrestrial – or earthly – bodies, making a comparison between the two.

But in verse 41 there is no such comparison.

In verse 40 the things peculiar to two distinct realms are compared, whereas in verse 41 only one of those realms is mentioned.

It is things unique to that – heavenly – realm alone that are contrasted. There is no reference to the terrestrial realm at all. Not a word concerning earthly bodies.

And if not, they do not enter into the equation. The comparison – in order to show the difference – is that of one heavenly body with another: the entire verse being concerned with the distinction between the glory of one heavenly body and that of another heavenly body: all the glory is in the heavens, the earth does not come into it.

In which case verse 41 is not only the fourth and last but it is equally a separate example from the three preceding instances.

The glory of the sun differs from the glory of the moon, differs from the glory of the stars, and the glory of one star differs from the glory of another star.

Well; but how does this exemplify the resurrection of the dead?

Because if there is such a multiplicity, variation, and complexity to the glory that shines in the heavens in that creation which waxeth old and is ready to vanish away, then, seeing that the LORD God Almighty has so great a glory to contrast, one form with another, in *this* creation, *how much more the everlasting glory of that which shall never decay, and cannot pass away, in the new creation of the world to come, whereof we speak?*

And, if so, in the resurrection from the dead.

Otherwise, why the *difference* in glory?

Because for all the differences in every glorious outshining throughout the heavens during the whole of time, put everything together, weigh the sum from the formation of the heavens till their dissolution, it is all no more than small dust in the balance compared to the glory that is yet to be revealed in the heavens that shall be created to suit the resurrection of the dead in glorious sonship.

But, at least, the difference–the astonishing difference–between one example of heavenly glory and another, must surely lead the mind to consider how much more an exceeding weight of glory pertains to that creation which still remains to be revealed, and that heaven which is yet to come.

And if yet to come, then in the resurrection of the dead.

Indeed, who but the most blinded fool can stand upon the earth, looking up into the heavens shining with glory, and not see what stares him in the face?

What? Then there is–and there *must be*–a resurrection from the dead for the world to come in consequence.

With such examples as these–as though he had enunciated no other doctrine!–well might Paul expostulate with the Corinthians from this cause alone 'Why should it be thought a thing incredible with you that God should raise the dead?', Acts 26:8.

Such examples themselves exclaim to them, Look up! Hearken!

For 'the heavens declare the glory of God; and the firmament showeth his handiwork. Day unto day uttereth speech, and night unto night showeth knowledge. There is no speech nor language, where their voice is not heard. Their line is gone out through all the earth, and their words to the end of the world', Psalm 19:1-4.

Surely this should have been their wisdom–over and above everything in Chapter 15 up to this point–that they should have looked up and seen–the witness being in their hearts–that in the resurrection from the dead 'they that be wise shall shine as the brightness of the firmament; and they that turn many to righteousness as the stars for ever and ever', Daniel 12:3.

For, 'Thou, Lord, in the beginning hast laid the foundation of the earth; and the heavens are the works of thine hands: they shall perish'–yea, and all the glory of them shall perish together–'but thou remainest; and they shall all wax old as doth a garment; and as a vesture shalt thou fold them up, and they shall be changed: but thou art the same, and thy years shall not fail', Hebrews 1:10-12.

Then, these things being so, the first creation having waxed old and vanished away, how much more shall the Maker of heaven and earth magnify his resplendent glory beyond all that eye hath seen, ear heard, or hath entered into the heart of man to conceive, in that new creation, that new heaven and new earth–the first heaven and the first earth having passed away– waiting to greet the saints in the glorious resurrection from the dead, world without end. Amen.

The apostle now proceeds to the brightness of that revelation of which the four preceding examples from creation were a pale reflection: 'So also is the resurrection of the dead.

'It is sown in corruption; it is raised in incorruption: it is sown in dishonour; it is raised in glory: it is sown in weakness; it is raised in power: it is sown a natural body; it is raised a spiritual body. There is a natural body, and there is a spiritual body', I Corinthians 15:42-44.

Just as previously from creation there were four examples of the resurrection from the dead, so now by revelation there are four applications of those examples, followed by the necessary conclusion.

Four times over what is sown is contrasted with what is raised. The dead, whether sown in corruption, dishonour, weakness, or 'nature'–ψυχικόν, *psuchikon*–in the resurrection are raised in incorruption, glory, power, and spirituality, respectively.

And what is sown? Why, 'a body'. And what is raised? Why, 'a *body*', I Corinthians 15:44. Not a *spirit*.

It may be *spiritual*, but *what* is spiritual is not *a* spirit. What is raised is that which was sown, namely *a body*, albeit a *spiritual* body.

That is, like unto 'his glorious body', Philippians 3:21, in which, however spiritual, he ate, drank, was handled, seen, was of flesh and bones, yet, nevertheless, was raised a *body* for the glorious inheritance of the everlasting kingdom in the new heaven *and the new earth* of which–his people having been raised in his likeness–*he* is the heir.

As to the resurrection of that people, they are raised to an inexpressible glory far transcending anything either imagined or dreamed of–let alone experienced–whilst in this body and in the present world.

No matter *how* much that which was glorious had appeared to the saints below, the glory to come surpasses all with a far more exceeding, consummate and everlasting brightness, beyond all precedent, even as the apostle had taught from the comparisons in the previous verses: '*So also* is the resurrection of the dead', verse 42.

The resurrection of the dead was *sown*. Four times over Paul stresses this.

But, like the seed which fell into the ground and died, what shall be raised *is not the same thing*. Yet, a glory once did indwell that which was sown.

Nevertheless for all that glory, for all that which had been, for all the having been the temple of the Holy Ghost; for all the abiding in Christ, and Christ abiding in us; for all the Father himself indwelling our spirit; for all the heavenly treasure within; still, that which had so glorious a habitation in the days of our pilgrimage never abode in anything more permanent than a fragile clay vessel.

Never more than a clay vessel: of itself it was ever the body of sin and death destined for the grave.

The apostle, full of glory, still called that in which the glory dwelt 'this vile body'.

It was still that in which inbred sin remained, inexorably to bring down the body into the decay of age, disease, wasting, and death.

This is that which was sown: buried in the earth. Covered over out of sight.

It is what was sown in corruption, soon to be forgotten, out of mind beneath the soil. Of these decomposing remains, rotting and mouldering, Job saith: 'they shall lie down alike in the dust, and the worms shall cover them', Job 21:26.

And again, 'worms destroy this body': here is the sowing in corruption, Job 19:26.

Nevertheless, for all this, it is still the body that was sown. And if so, neither death, nor the grave, nor yet so ignominious a dissolution, can possibly prove to be the end. The end, that is, of the *body* that was sown.

As the body is sown in corruption, so in like manner it is sown in dishonour. Once comely, now corrupt; once had in honour, now sown in dishonour. No sooner the shadow of death passes over the features, but the cold hand of death closes over the corpse.

87

Now men avert their faces, who had once paid honour in the land of the living.

The soul having departed, how soon is comeliness turned to corruption, honour into dishonour.

How quickly the swiftly putrefying cadaver must be buried in the ground, the stink of death already tainting the air. This is to be sown in dishonour.

It is also to be sown in weakness. The life may have clung, held on with desperation, even to the very last. But loose its hold it must.

The strong, the mighty man, the valiant, all alike succumb to the king of terrors, and there is no escaping the inevitable departure of the soul from the body, no, not though one had in life the vigour of ten men.

When the grim reaper calls, the strength ebbs away, the life departs, the soul leaves the body, and nothing but the empty shell remains, so soon to turn to dust. This is called 'sown in weakness'.

It is to be sown a natural—*psuchikon*—body.

Natural? That is, shapen in iniquity; conceived in sin. Born in the man of sin and death. Belonging to the earth, earthy; under the curse, beneath the Fall. Of this present passing world. Doomed to decay and death.

That is what is 'natural' to man in the age that now is: the sentence already passed, the process of inbred sin and inherent dissolution at work even from conception, the passing of time inexorably sapping the life, until death parts soul and body: this is to be sown a natural body!

The degradation of this sowing under the ghastly hand of death is indicated by the grisly consequences of corruption, dishonour, weakness, and the immutable law of nature universally evident in all creation, namely – far from the theoretic fiction of evolution – the reality of decline and dissolution.

So soon! Martha knew this, and, when the Lord called for the grave of Lazarus to be opened, cried out in horror, 'Lord, by this time he stinketh: for he hath been dead four days', John 11:39.

But out of corruption, dishonour, weakness, and natural decay, Lazarus was chosen to show in a figure the raising to incorruption, the resurrection of glory, the rising again in power, and the certain promise of a spiritual body.

'Said I not unto thee, that, if thou wouldest believe, thou shouldest see the glory of God?', John 11:40.

Of this sowing in death, and raising to glory, through Christ the firstfruits, called, 'the Resurrection and the Life' – in whom, believing, though one were dead, yet shall one live – Peter speaks on the day of Pentecost, citing the case of David:

'Men and brethren, let me freely speak unto you of the patriarch David, that he is both dead and buried, and his sepulchre is with us unto this day.

'Therefore being a prophet, and knowing that God had sworn with an oath to him, that of the fruit of his loins, according to the flesh, he would raise up Christ to sit on his throne; he seeing this before spake of the resurrection of Christ, that *his* soul was not left in *hadēs*, neither *his* flesh did see corruption.

'This Jesus hath God raised up, whereof we all are witnesses', Acts 2:29-32.

Now, *here* is the Resurrection and the Life, even the firstfruits of them that slept.

Of this the apostle Paul speaks likewise, saying, 'David, after he had served his own generation by the will of God, fell on sleep, and was laid unto his fathers, and saw corruption: but he, whom God raised again, saw no corruption', Acts 13:36,37.

Yes, David saw corruption, together with all the saints which have been since the world began: their bodies, one and all, were sown in corruption.

But he whom God raised from the dead, Christ the firstfruits, saw no corruption, even as David prophesied some one thousand years before: 'For thou wilt not leave my soul in *sheol*; neither wilt thou suffer thine Holy One to see corruption', Psalm 16:10.

But *we* see corruption. Our body is sown in corruption; it is sown in dishonour; it is sown in weakness; it is sown a natural body.

A natural *dead* body.

Death cuts off all life, all honour, all strength, all that stands this side of the grave, shutting us up to revolting putrescence and decomposition, so soon to be forgotten in the darkness of the tomb, in which nothing is heard but the soft falling of decay.

If so, What a terrible enemy death proves to be: indeed, it is the last enemy.

When death strikes its mortal blow, it shall not strike again. The worst possible fears are realized, and the ultimate finality is foreclosed. Oh, death is the *last* enemy, with a witness.

But now is Christ risen from the dead, and become the first-fruits of them that slept.

As to the last enemy, 'the last enemy *that shall be destroyed* is death', I Corinthians 15:26. 'So also is the resurrection of the dead.

'It is sown in corruption; *it is raised in incorruption*: it is sown in dishonour; *it is raised in glory*: it is sown in weakness; *it is raised in power*: it is sown a natural body; *it is raised a spiritual body*', I Corinthians 15:42-44.

What then shall we say to these things? We shall echo with Paul, '*Death is swallowed up in victory*', I Corinthians 15:54.

Wherefore observe that in each of the four instances, the very use of the word 'sown'–though what immediately precedes and for a season follows the sowing were never so ignominious–fills every soul in Christ with hope. Because sowing predicates hope. Hope of rising again. Of the *body* rising again.

And of that body which shall rise again–which was sown in death–the apostle declares in the first of four instances: '*It* is sown in corruption; *it* is raised in incorruption', I Corinthians 15:42.

Where that which was sown is the opposite in character to that which shall be raised.

What shall be raised is *incapable of decay*. If so, *it can never die again*: 'Christ being raised from the dead dieth no more'–and neither do those in Christ, who are raised in incorruption– 'death hath no more dominion over him', Romans 6:9, and neither hath it over those in Christ, who are raised incorruptible.

Mark well that in this place–indeed in the whole of I Corinthians 15:42-44–Paul is not referring to the *soul*. It is not *that* that is 'sown'. It is the *body* that is 'sown'. The apostle refers to *the body*: '*It* is sown in corruption; *it* is raised in incorruption.'

Therefore in the resurrection there shall be an entire transformation. Nevertheless it is certain that–though radically transformed–*the body that shall be raised is the body that was sown*.

But raised 'incorruptible': '*it* is raised in incorruption', I Corinthians 15:42.

It is raised immortal, imperishable; it is raised with an inherent incapacity of decay; it is undying: in a word, it is raised 'incorruptible'.

To this end, whilst yet in the present corruption, the saints lived: and 'to them who by patient continuance in well doing' —despite all the weight and impediment of this corruptible body— 'seek for glory and honour and *immortality*'—this last being the same word in the Greek as that translated 'incorruption', I Corinthians 15:42—God, 'who will render to every man according to his deeds' will most assuredly render to all such saints 'eternal life', Romans 2:6,7.

Doubtless this entails the fight of faith, and at that against a veritable Goliath of an enemy, namely, the intrusive cloddishness of this heavy clay that so often weighs the soul down to earth with sighing and despondency.

Nevertheless the constant battle against carnal ease and indulgence is not much more than that which is required of athletes, who, to win the crown, must make consistent and painful sacrifices in the endeavour.

'Now they do it to obtain a corruptible crown; but we an *incorruptible*.

'I therefore so run, not as uncertainly; so fight I, not as one that beateth the air: but I keep under my body, and bring it into subjection', I Corinthians 9:25-27. 'If by any means I might attain unto the resurrection of the dead', Philippians 3:11.

And why not, seeing that we have been saved 'and called with an holy calling, not according to our works, but according to his own purpose and grace, which was given us in Christ Jesus before the world began, but is now made manifest by the appearing of our Saviour Jesus Christ, *who hath abolished death, and hath brought life and immortality*'—it is the same Greek word— '*to light through the gospel*', II Timothy 1:9,10.

This is the light of the heavenly vision that illuminates the heart of his people, every one of whom sets his countenance steadfastly towards Zion, looking for the resurrection of the body from the dead at the return of the Lord, to be raised in incorruption.

But for what, such an undying body, incapable of decay, save to live for ever, and to live for ever *in that body*.

To what end? To the end of 'an inheritance *incorruptible*, and undefiled, and that fadeth not away, reserved in heaven for you, who are kept by the power of God through faith unto salvation ready to be revealed in the last time', I Peter 1:4,5.

'Now unto the King eternal, *immortal*' – it is the same Greek word – 'invisible, the only wise God, be honour and glory for ever and ever. Amen', I Timothy 1:17.

Secondly, 'It is sown in dishonour; it is raised in glory', I Corinthians 15:43. But though the body should be sown in dishonour, yet, Christ being in the saints, 'the body is dead because of sin; but the Spirit is life because of righteousness', Romans 8:10.

In this life they had reckoned themselves 'dead indeed unto sin, but alive unto God through Jesus Christ our Lord', Romans 6:11.

They had counted themselves 'crucified with Christ', Galatians 2:20. Hence therefore, despite this vile body, soon to be sown in dishonour, they had 'lived unto God', so that they passed the time of their sojourning here in fear, 'by patient continuance in well doing' – in *this* life – 'seeking for *glory*' – in *that* life which is to come, Romans 2:7.

Nor shall they be disappointed: for though this vile body were 'sown in dishonour', beyond all question it shall be 'raised in glory' at the coming of Christ and the resurrection of the dead.

And what glory! 'For our conversation'–even now–'is in heaven; from whence also we look for the Saviour, the Lord Jesus Christ: who shall *change* our vile body'–so dishonourable in its sowing: so inglorious–'that it may be fashioned'–in the resurrection, when that which was sown is raised in glory–'*like unto his glorious body*', Philippians 3:20,21.

Like unto *his* glorious body? What likeness is that?

This was shown at the transfiguration, when 'he was transfigured before them: and his face did shine as the sun, and his raiment was white as the light', Matthew 17:2. Like that: his glorious body is like that; *and our body of glory will be like unto it.*

Again; 'He was transfigured before them. And his raiment became shining, exceeding white as snow; so as no fuller on earth can white them', Mark 9:2,3.

Like that: 'like unto *his* glorious body.'

Once more; 'And as he prayed, the fashion of his countenance was altered, and his raiment was white and glistering', Luke 9:29.

Altered, yes, as a foretaste of the glory that was to come; and we too, who are of his body, in Christ, likewise, 'we shall be changed' in the resurrection of the dead to everlasting glory.

What glory! 'And as he journeyed, he came near Damascus: and suddenly there shined round about him a light from heaven', Acts 9:3.

Whence the light? From a *person*. A glorified *person* in heaven. For the *person* gave forth the radiance: 'I am Jesus', came the voice of him who shone with such glory.

Again; 'And it came to pass, that, as I made my journey, and was come nigh unto Damascus about noon, suddenly there shone from heaven a great light round about me', Acts 22:6.

This was the glory of the Lord, raised from the dead, ascended into heaven. Concerning which glory it is said of all those raised in his likeness, 'like unto'.

Once more; 'At midday, O king, I saw in the way a light from heaven, above the brightness of the sun, shining round about me', Acts 26:13. This was the light that shone so brightly from the glorified Son in heaven.

But in that day this light shall not only shine *round about* Paul: raised from the dead in the body of glory, the light shall shine *in* him, and *through* him, in glorious radiance, world without end.

And not Paul only, but likewise all those that love his appearing, as it is written, 'Christ the firstfruits; afterward they that are Christ's at his coming', I Corinthians 15:23.

And as is the firstfruits, so also shall be the harvest. Glorious. Glorified. Like that.

Though the body *was* sown in dishonour; *it is raised in glory*. *That* kind of glory: everlasting glory. The glory of the Son: 'like unto *his* glorious body, according to the working whereby he is able even to subdue all things unto himself', Philippians 3:21.

Thirdly: 'It is sown in weakness; it is raised in power', I Corinthians 15:43.

Observe the wording, 'sown in weakness'. There is nothing weaker than a dying man. None so weak as one on his death bed. No weakness like that of the last gasping breath, trailing into the expiry of the final dwindling sigh.

And then, what is weaker than the limp, lifeless, inert corpse, ready to be interred in the grave? That is to be sown in weakness indeed.

95

So weak! Then how wonderful it is that *this*–no matter how long the weakness of what was sown moulders beneath the earth– *this* is that which is to be 'raised in power'.

If so, there is no power, but absolutely no power, like that of the resurrection from the dead, 'When the Son of man shall come in his glory, and all the holy angels with him', Matthew 25:31. No wonder that 'with great power gave the apostles witness of the resurrection of the Lord Jesus', Acts 4:33.

Then how much more certainly of *all* the dead? 'Marvel not at this: for the hour is coming, in the which *all* that are in the graves shall hear his voice, and shall come forth; they that have done good, unto the resurrection of life; and they that have done evil, unto the resurrection of damnation', John 5:28,29.

It is not that the resurrection is anything other than a *proven, witnessed fact*, testified by the raising of Christ from the dead, and in the signs that followed:

'And the graves were opened; and many bodies'–mark that: *bodies*–'of the saints which slept arose, and came out of the graves after his resurrection, and went into the holy city, *and appeared unto many*', Matthew 27:52,53.

The Son does not raise *ghosts*; observe, it says '*many bodies*' were raised from the dead, 'and *appeared unto many*'.

These '*many*' were contemporaries of Matthew: *he would never have written this without the certainty that none of the 'many' either would or could deny or ridicule the record of what they themselves had witnessed with their own eyes, and to which they had testified with their own mouths.*

Why should it be thought a thing incredible with you that God should raise the dead? He *did* raise the dead, and he *will* raise the dead. Even before his own resurrection Jesus heaped scorn upon those fools who scoffed *at so obvious and palpable a fact*:

96

'Do ye not therefore err, because ye know not the scriptures, neither the power of God?'–they were without excuse: they *had* the scriptures; they ought to have known them.

They *knew* of the power of God; they ought not to have limited that power, much less dismissed its exercise in relation to the resurrection at the last day–'For when they shall rise from the dead, they neither marry, nor are given in marriage; but are as the angels which are in heaven.

'And as touching the dead, that they rise: have ye not read in the book of Moses, how in the bush God spake unto him, saying, I am the God of Abraham, and the God of Isaac, and the God of Jacob? He is not the God of the dead, but the God of the living: ye therefore do greatly err', Mark 12:24-27.

Greatly err, because when God testified to Moses, *I am*–not *I was*–the God of Abraham, Isaac, and Jacob, he bore testimony to three men who had died *hundreds of years before*. But he was *still* their God: then their souls lived on, for it is certain that he is not the God of the dead, but of the living.

And if living at *that* time, when Jesus spoke, then, equally, their God *now also*, centuries and millennia making no difference to the God of glory, nor to the power of the living God.

And if he was the God of their living souls for so long a time, do you think that God by Jesus Christ will not raise them up in their bodies at the resurrection in the last day?

What, when Jesus testified 'Abraham'–note that name: *Abraham*, whose body had died millennia before–'Abraham rejoiced to see my day: and he saw it, and was glad.

'Then said the Jews unto him, Thou art not yet fifty years old, and hast thou seen Abraham? Jesus said unto them, Verily, verily, I say unto you, before Abraham was, I am', John 8:56-58.

Then do you suppose that Abraham shall not rise in the harvest at the end of the world, when Christ the firstfruits comes for his own?

What? not raise Abraham's body, and that of all the saints, when, just before raising Lazarus from the dead, in an open and public resurrection before multitudes – all of whom knew that Lazarus had been dead and buried, with putrefaction set in, these four days past – Jesus declared of himself what he was about to demonstrate to them all:

'I am the resurrection, and the life: he that believeth in me, *though he were dead*, yet shall he live: and whosoever liveth and believeth in me shall never die. Believest thou this?', John 11:25,26.

Believe? But they *saw* it: 'He cried with a loud voice, Lazarus, come forth. And he that was dead came forth, bound hand and foot with graveclothes: and his face was bound about with a napkin. Jesus said unto them, Loose him, and let him go', John 11:43,44.

This was the power of his resurrection, and every one of his saints shall experience its full magnitude, from the beginning of the world to the end of it, in the day of his coming to raise the dead.

Of this the Holy Ghost bears witness within, according to the scriptures and the power of God, even now fulfilling the prayers of the apostle Paul, as it is written,

'That the God of our Lord Jesus Christ, the Father of glory, may give unto you the spirit of wisdom and revelation in the knowledge of him: the eyes of your understanding being enlightened; that ye may know what is the hope of his calling, and what the riches of the glory of his inheritance in the saints,

'And *what the exceeding greatness of his power to usward who believe, according to the working of his mighty power, which he wrought in Christ, when he raised him from the dead, and set him at his own right hand in the heavenlies'*, Ephesians 1:17-20.

Now, *that* is the power to raise what had been sown in weakness, a power *absolutely* certain in the resurrection of every one that believeth.

'Why should it be thought a thing incredible with you, that God should raise the dead?', Acts 26:8. What! In the teeth of the scriptures, and of the power of God?

'The hand of the LORD was upon me, and carried me out in the spirit of the LORD, and set me down in the midst of the valley which was full of bones, and caused me to pass by them round about:

'And, behold, there were very many in the open valley; and, lo, they were very dry.

'And he said unto me, Son of man, can these bones live? And I answered, O Lord GOD, thou knowest.

'Again he said unto me, Prophesy upon these bones, and say unto them, O ye dry bones, hear the word of the LORD. Thus saith the Lord GOD unto these bones; Behold, I will cause breath to enter into you, and ye shall live:

'And I will lay sinews upon you, and will bring up flesh upon you, and cover you with skin, and put breath in you, and ye shall live; and ye shall know that I am the LORD.

'So I prophesied as I was commanded: and as I prophesied, there was a noise, and behold a shaking, and the bones came together, bone to his bone.

'And when I beheld, lo, the sinews and the flesh came up upon them, and the skin covered them above: but there was no breath in them.

'Then said he unto me, Prophesy unto the wind, prophesy, son of man, and say to the wind, Thus saith the Lord GOD; Come from the four winds, O breath, and breathe upon these slain, that they may live.

'So I prophesied as he commanded me, and the breath came into them, and they lived, and stood up upon their feet, an exceeding great army', Ezekiel 37:1-10.

Yes, *'it is raised in power'*. Power to join bone to bone; power to fetch bones from the depths of the earth, from the bottom of the sea; from the utmost ends of the world.

Power to gather scattered dust, imperishable substance, indestructible matter, irreducible elements, from the bodies of all mankind since the foundation of the earth till the day of its dissolution: the *same* matter.

O, ye do greatly err, knowing neither the scriptures, nor the power of God.

'And I saw a great white throne, and him that sat on it, from whose face the earth and the heaven fled away; and there was found no place for them.

'And I saw the dead, small and great, stand before God; and the books were opened: and another book was opened, which is the book of life:

'And the dead were judged out of those things which were written in the books, according to their works.

'*And the sea gave up the dead which were in it; and death and hadēs delivered up the dead which were in them: and they were judged every man according to their works.*

'And death and *hadēs* were cast into the lake of fire. This is the second death. And whosoever was not found written in the book of life was cast into the lake of fire', Revelation 20:11-15.

Now, this is being sown in weakness but raised in power with a witness.

And how say some among you that there is no resurrection of the dead? Then, your faith is vain, and ye are yet in your sins. But now *is* Christ risen from the dead, and become the firstfruits of them that slept.

Fourthly, 'It is sown a natural body; it is raised a spiritual body', I Corinthians 15:44.

'It is sown a natural body.' This is that body which Paul calls 'our vile body'. It is conceived in sin, saith David, and shapen in iniquity. It is the body of sin, declares the apostle. It is born in sin, and hath the sentence of death in itself.

As with all natural things, it is subject to decay; is a seedbed of corruption; leads to groaning and travail; sickness and disease; and ends its meaningless existence in disillusioned vanity upon the death bed.

Thence, it is said to be 'sown'. That is, buried under the earth in death.

Yet what a glorious promise awaits all who 'fell asleep' in Christ. Though, like others, their body was sown a natural body, yet *their* existence here was not meaningless, neither were *their* years on earth spent in wasting and vanity.

By patient continuance in well doing they sought for glory and honour and immortality, confessing themselves to be strangers and pilgrims upon the earth, looking for a better resurrection, a heavenly country, and a city which hath foundations, whose builder and maker is God.

And thus seeking, so looking, they fell asleep in Christ, their souls departing to be with him for ever. But as to their bodies, each one, Paul declares, 'it is sown a natural body'.

101

Yes, but 'it' – mark that: *it* – 'it is raised a spiritual body.' Not 'it is raised a spirit', observe. God forbid! It – *it*, notice – 'it is raised a spiritual *body*.'

There is nothing ephemeral, nothing ghostly, about that: a spirit is a spirit is a spirit. What is spiritual is spiritual is spiritual. And a body is a body is a body. Then a spiritual body is a spiritual body is a spiritual *body*. And nothing less.

A *body* was sown, but having a certain nature. *That body* shall be raised, *having a different nature altogether*. But *still*, a body. Only, a body suited to the divine nature – for God is a Spirit, John 4:24 – namely, a spiritual body, raised to abide in him, and for his indwelling, with all saints, to the endless ages of everlasting glory.

But some man will say, A spiritual *body* is a contradiction in terms, and therefore, since it is spiritual, the resurrection cannot be of the *body*, much less that corpse which was buried in the grave.

Against such vain and godless theorizing, which, whilst boasting of itself as 'reason', actually intrudes into things which it has neither seen nor can see, having the temerity to speculate about dimensions beyond human capacity even to imagine, it is no wonder to discover that the apostle protests with withering scorn, 'Thou fool', I Corinthians 15:36.

A spiritual body a contradiction in terms? Then I will contradict the terms of such folly with the facts and evidence of the spiritual body, once having been sown in death – and at that, the ignominious death of the cross, where the Saviour, being made sin and bearing sins, was crucified under wrath and the curse – was thereafter raised from the dead by the glory of the Father, and 'was seen many days of them which came up with him from Galilee to Jerusalem, who are his witnesses unto the people', Acts 13:31.

102

That is, so seen many days after – mark that: *after* – 'God raised him from the dead', Acts 13:30.

If such a fool should continue his palpable contradictions and say, But that was the Lord: whereas 'raised a spiritual body' refers to the saints, I Corinthians 15:44, I answer, Yes, the Corinthian text does refer to the saints; in that saidst thou truly.

Wherein thou liest, however, lurks hidden beneath the sly insinuation that *the resurrection of the body of the Lord, and that of his own, is different.* But the apostle declares, 'For if we have been planted together in the likeness of his death, we shall be also in the likeness of his resurrection', Romans 6:5.

And again, he 'shall *change*' – not *eliminate*; it says *change* – 'our vile body, that it' – *it*, mark that, *it* – 'may be fashioned' – *fashioned*, notice: Greek, *having the same form with* – 'fashioned *like unto his glorious body*', Philippians 3:21.

Now where is the difference?

And where is your folly? Why, it is sunk like lead in the mired and dirty waters of your unbelief: 'The wicked are like the troubled sea, when it cannot rest, whose waters cast up mire and dirt. There is no peace, saith my God, to the wicked', Isaiah 57:20,21.

As to the spiritual body being, first, a *body* notwithstanding; and, second, answering to the resurrection – though changed – of *that body which was sown*: Consider:

Firstly, since *it* – the body – of the saints that is to be raised at his coming is in the likeness of *his* resurrection, and since it is fashioned *like unto* his glorious body, *it follows of necessity that it is a body notwithstanding, for all that it is a spiritual body.*

For its being *spiritual* does not, and cannot, nullify its being a *body.*

'And as they' – to whom the Lord had appeared, risen from the dead – 'thus spake, Jesus himself stood in the midst of them.' He had appeared bodily to two of them; yet he had vanished out of their sight. Then *here* is a spiritual body; it belonged to and was capable of spiritual dimensions beyond understanding.

Thereupon the Lord appeared bodily to all of them, suddenly materializing in their midst: now this defies all imagination; but what *cannot* be denied is the *fact that in that spiritual body he did so, witness the testimony of the apostles.*

'Jesus himself' – *himself*, mark – 'stood in the midst of them, and saith unto them, Peace be unto you.

'But they were terrified and affrighted, and supposed that they had seen a spirit' – that is, a ghost – 'And he said unto them, Why are ye troubled? and why do thoughts arise in your hearts?

'Behold my hands and my feet, that it is *I myself: handle me, and see;* for a spirit *hath not flesh and bones, as ye see me have.'*

If so, his risen body, of flesh and bones, was for all that *a spiritual body.* But, despite that it was spiritual, *it was still corporeal and could be handled.* In a word, it *was* a body. And, recognizably, *his* body. Yet a *spiritual* body.

'And when he had thus spoken, he showed them his hands and his feet. And while they yet believed not for joy, and wondered, he said unto them, Have ye here any meat?

'And they gave him a piece of a broiled fish, and of an honey-comb. And he took it, and did eat before them.'

Then that is the end of all controversy. It was *him*. In *his body*. But raised *such a spiritual body that it had those distinct characteristics.* See Luke 24:36-43.

And as is the firstfruits, so shall be the harvest.

Secondly, carefully notice that – whether the Lord, or they that are his at his coming – it *is* that body which was sown. 'But Thomas, one of the twelve, called Didymus, was not with them when Jesus came. The other disciples therefore said unto him, We have seen the Lord.

'But he said unto them, Except I shall see in his hands the print of the nails, and put my finger into the print of the nails, and thrust my hand into his side, I will not believe.

'And after eight days again his disciples were within, and Thomas with them: then came Jesus, the doors being shut'–now, *that* manifestation was *spiritual*; yes: but it was *still his body*–'and stood in the midst, and said, Peace be unto you.

'Then saith he to Thomas, Reach hither thy finger, and behold my hands; and reach hither thy hand, and thrust it into my side: and be not faithless, but believing.

'And Thomas answered and said unto him, My Lord and my God.

'Jesus saith unto him, Thomas, because thou hast seen me, thou hast believed: blessed are they that have not seen, and yet have believed', John 20:24-29.

Now this spiritual body, materializing in their midst, was beyond any shadow of doubt *that in which he had been crucified*. That which was dead three days in the tomb. That which, raised from the dead by the glory of the Father, yet bore the print of the nails and the wound of the spear.

Then, as for us also, *it* is sown a natural body; yes, and *it* is raised a spiritual body.

'There is a natural body, and there is a spiritual body', I Corinthians 15:44.

The natural body is of the earth; it belongs to this world; it pertains to the present age; it is born, grows, withers, and dies, in a moment, a span of time; its generation is of the man of sin and death; it is in the Fall, under the curse, and of the flesh; it is rooted in Adam's transgression, and doomed to dissolution.

Yes, there is a natural body. But thanks be unto God, which giveth us the victory through our Lord Jesus Christ, *there is a spiritual body*.

The spiritual body is for the world to come; it is for the saints' rest; it is for the eternal inheritance; it belongs to the new heaven and the new earth; it pertains to the holy city, new Jerusalem, which comes down from God out of heaven; it is for everlasting bliss in the glorious inheritance promised in Christ before the world began, and entered into when the world is no more.

'There is a spiritual body.' It is for God, to abide in him, and he in us, in Father, Son, and Holy Ghost, world without end, manifesting forth his glory.

God is love; God is light; God is a Spirit. And, in that spiritual *body*, in the inheritance of *the world to come*, the light, life, and love of God shall radiate in and through that spiritual body, world without end. Amen.

'There is a spiritual body': it is divine, for God is a Spirit. It is heavenly, for we shall bear the image of the heavenly. It is glorious, for it is fashioned like unto his glorious body. It is everlasting, for evermore to radiate the indwelling of eternal life.

It is incorruptible, for it is not possible that it should decay. It is immortal, for it is incapable of dying. It is spiritual, for it is agreeable to the divine nature, for ever to worship in spirit and in truth.

O, mark well, all ye who are of the chosen generation, the heirs of promise, who are of faith, the sons of God, for to you the word is certain, and the promise is sure, world without end, as the Spirit and the truth bear witness: 'There *is* a spiritual body', I Corinthians 15:44.

The folly of questioning the resurrection of the dead has been shown from Creation, I Corinthians 15:35-41, followed by the revelation made manifest through the pen of the apostle, verses 42-44. This passage is the first part of the revelation. Paul now continues with the second and last part, verses 45-50.

'So also it has been written, The first man Adam became a living soul; the last Adam a quickening spirit. But not first the spiritual, but the natural, then the spiritual: the first man out of the earth, made of dust; the second man the Lord out of heaven.

'Such as he made of dust, such also those made of dust; and such as the heavenly [one], such also the heavenly [ones].

'And according as we bore the image of the [one] made of dust, we shall bear also the image of the heavenly [one]. But this I say, brethren, that flesh and blood cannot inherit [the] kingdom of God, nor does corruption inherit incorruption', I Corinthians 15:45-50.

As before, this rendering – which I consider far and away superior – is taken from 'The Greek-English New Testament', Bagster, 1877.

However, I refer the reader to the Authorized Version, only with the cautionary admonition to make a comparison with the passage quoted from Bagster – in order to ascertain the original – where this is necessary. 'And this will we do, if God permit', Hebrews 6:3.

'And so it is written, The first man Adam was made a living soul; the last Adam was made a quickening spirit.' So the Authorized Version.

The alternative interlinear reading, literally translating the same – and peerless – Received Greek Text, renders this verse: 'So also it has been written, The first man Adam became a living soul; the last Adam a quickening spirit', I Corinthians 15:45.

From which we are to observe that all that is begotten after the flesh – man, woman, and child: born, begetting, dying – springs from one single progenitor, Adam.

But for all the appearances in the world, he is not the *only* Adam, nor is he the *only* progenitor, in the mind, will, counsel, and purpose of God.

Though every living soul – in every dying body – may be all that is visible on earth, populating the world, *more exists that pertains to the world to come than is visible to earthly sight*.

That is, there is a *first* Adam, yes, *but there is also a last Adam*.

And these two are essentially, radically, and absolutely different the one from the other. Furthermore, what Paul is about to reveal is this: *so also are their respective posterities*.

One Adam, the first, begat after himself. Such living souls– having the sentence of death in themselves – constitute all that is to be seen of mankind throughout the whole world, in every generation, and among all nations.

This is visible humanity, the sum of all living souls begotten after the flesh by natural generation. But – as is evident from the first Adam – such living souls, together with those that begat them, and every one begotten by them, spend their fleeting days in corruptible bodies, destined for death and the grave.

Despite the appearance of vigour and growth this sentence of death is just as true at conception, birth, growth, and in youth.

All descend from the first Adam, who was made a living soul from the dust of the ground by the breath of the LORD God, as it is written, 'And the LORD God formed man of the dust of the ground, and breathed into his nostrils the breath of life; and man became a living soul', Genesis 2:7.

Thus Adam was made a living soul by God, but he became the man of sin and death by himself.

And after himself he begat his posterity, which, according to the flesh, has multiplied and does multiply, generation after generation from the beginning until now, being that humanity, the only humanity, dying humanity – the living soul descending after death into *sheol* or *hadēs* – seen upon earth.

But it is not the only humanity, nor is the first Adam the only Adam, seen before God in heaven.

Because there is *another* Adam, the *last* Adam, called 'a quickening spirit', seated in the glory of heaven, who, with *his* posterity, is heir of the world to come by the resurrection from the dead.

The former is that to which Paul referred when he said, 'The first man Adam became a living soul'; even as he had declared before, 'For as in Adam all die', I Corinthians 15:22.

The latter is that to which the apostle points when he says, 'the last Adam a quickening spirit', which finds its responsive expression in I Corinthians 15:22 with the words 'even so in Christ shall all be made alive'.

'The last Adam a quickening spirit': observe that the Holy Ghost sets 'the last Adam' over against – and in contrast with – 'the first Adam'.

Many unspiritual, uninspired, and ignorant persons – not to mention so-called Hymn writers – misrepresent Christ by calling him 'the second Adam'. Not so the apostle Paul. He is definitive: the Son of God is 'the last Adam', not the second; *the last.*

There is not another: after the *last* there can be no other. There is no such thing as 'a second Adam'.

The *last* Adam, in terms of his being 'a quickening spirit', is the consummation of the purpose of God, the fulfilment of all things, the beginning of *everlasting* glory.

The Holy Ghost reveals him as the last Adam, and as the second man, in contrast with the first Adam, the first man.

If 'the last *Adam*', then Headship is postulated.

If the first man Adam is reckoned as the head and progenitor of that seed which–subsequent to his transgression and becoming the man of sin and death–issued forth from him, *then this is equally true of the last Adam, the head of that progeny–he having wrought righteousness and ascended on high–begotten in him.* Hence the first man Adam is referred to as 'the figure of him that was to come', Romans 5:14.

But who was to come? Why, the last Adam, a quickening spirit.

Romans 5:12-21 contrasts the two men; their two acts; the judgment of God upon those acts; the consequences of that judgment; and the effect of this upon the two seeds respectively.

This doctrine is stated in order to reveal the truth of the Reconciliation, or, as it ought to have been translated, the Substitution.

However, whilst taking up the truth of the first Adam and the last, I Corinthians 15:45 does so in relation to the resurrection of the dead.

Nevertheless Headship, which appears in Adam consequent to the bringing in of sin and death after the Fall, proceeds in Christ subsequent to his death and resurrection from the ascension.

Then, '*the last Adam, a quickening spirit*', refers to the Son of God in glory following the completion and vindication of his work on earth.

And if the Son is the last Adam from the glorious ascension, then he is so above the heavens, whence all the favour of God that proceeds from him, namely, his work; the judgment of God upon that work; the consequences of that judgment; with the assured fulfilment in grace of every promise, appears established and secure to all his seed.

What favour exactly? What consequences precisely? Those of 'a quickening spirit'.

Note that he is 'a quickening spirit' in terms of being the last Adam, a unique name, and one exclusive to the context of I Corinthians 15. If so, of the resurrection of the dead in Christ.

The meaning is obvious: the last Adam quickens, and he quickens spiritually, a conclusion inherent in the title 'a quickening spirit'. But who and what does he quicken? The answer is contextually indisputable: he quickens his saints, and he quickens their dead bodies.

This quickening begins inwardly in his people on earth. Such an interior work is expounded and enlarged under the title 'Quickening' in my book 'Saving Faith', which the reader would do well to ponder with diligence.

However, in I Corinthians 15:45, quickening is in the context of *the dead bodies of the saints*, and is that which is to be wrought in virtue of the office of the Son of God as The Last Adam: *thus* he is 'a quickening spirit' in the resurrection of the mortal remains of every one of his own people, as it is written, 'Blessed are the dead which die in the Lord from henceforth', Revelation 14:13.

111

The word 'quickening' – *zōopoieō* – occurs some twelve times in the new testament, and the majority of these occurrences refers to the Son of God quickening *the buried bodies* of his own people in the resurrection from the dead.

For example, 'As in Adam all die, even so in Christ shall all' – the dead in Christ – 'be made alive', I Corinthians 15:22, where 'made alive' is *zōopoieō*, 'quicken', or, grammatically, in this case, 'be quickened'.

Again, 'For as the Father raiseth up *the dead*, and *quickeneth them*; even so the Son *quickeneth* whom he will', John 5:21.

Once more, 'God' – is he – 'who *quickeneth* the dead, and calleth those things which be not as though they were', Romans 4:17. What things? Why, the bodies of the saints in the coming resurrection of the dead.

Certainly, this is a thing which 'is not'; and yet God speaks about it 'as though it were': 'For the vision is for an appointed time, but at the end it shall speak, and not lie: though it tarry, wait for it; because it will surely come, it will not tarry', Habakkuk 2:3.

Another example: 'But if the Spirit of him that raised up Jesus from the dead dwell in you, he that raised up Christ from *the dead* shall also *quicken* your *mortal bodies* by his Spirit that dwelleth in you', Romans 8:11.

Quicken your mortal bodies? Yes, for 'this mortal must put on immortality', I Corinthians 15:53.

Does anyone doubt this? 'Thou fool, that which thou sowest is not *quickened*, except it die', I Corinthians 15:36.

'Marvel not at this: for the hour is coming, in the which *all that are in the graves shall'* – shall, shall – '*hear his voice, and shall come forth; they that have done good, unto the resurrection of life*', John 5:28,29.

'Jesus said unto her, I'–the last Adam, a quickening spirit–'am the resurrection and the life: he that believeth in me, *though he were dead*, yet shall he live', John 11:25.

Live? Yes, live again *in the body*, in the resurrection of the dead, which the raising of Lazarus, who had believed on him, yet had died, and lain four days in the grave, proved infallibly, demonstrating in a figure the coming resurrection of the dead.

Now this is the certain destiny, and it will be the sure accomplishment, of 'the last Adam, a quickening spirit', I Corinthians 15:45; whence, therefore, the name, the office, and the description.

'Howbeit that was not first which is spiritual, but that which is natural; and afterward that which is spiritual', I Corinthians 15:46, Authorized Version.

Translating the same Received Text–the *only* safe Greek Text, largely ignored by and since the Revised Version, 1881, when the fallacious Westcott and Hort text became the basis for modern translations– the thoroughly sound interlinear –and literal– translation of 'The Englishman's Greek-English New Testament', 1877, renders this verse as follows: 'But not first the spiritual, but the natural, then the spiritual.'

Not first the spiritual? No. Adam came first, and hence the natural man is called 'the first man Adam', who was made a living soul.

Afterwards came Christ, a life-giving spirit, declared to be the Son of God with power, according to the Spirit of holiness, by the resurrection from the dead, Romans 1:4.

Hence, 'afterward that which is spiritual.'

The Authorized Version continues, 'the first man is of the earth, earthy: the second man is the Lord from heaven', verse 47, but this does not at all translate the Greek: it confounds the Greek.

113

'The Englishman's Greek-English New Testament' of 1877 is different: it clarifies the Greek. Quote: 'The first man out of the earth, made of dust; the second man the Lord out of heaven.'

The Authorized states 'of the earth, earthy' but the Greek is composed of quite different words: first, γῆς, *gēs*, the appropriate grammatical form of γῆ, *gē*, earth. The next word *in the Greek text* is χοϊκός, *choikos*, meaning – in this grammatical form – 'of the dust'.

Two entirely distinct Greek words, rendered – in effect, so as to hide the difference from the reader – by one and the same English word in the Authorized Version.

But the difference between the two Greek words is distinguished precisely by the Greek-English New Testament of 1877, namely, quote: 'of the *earth*, made of *dust*.' For Adam, of the earth, *was* made of dust. And so are we. For unto fallen Adam the LORD God said, Genesis 3:19, 'dust thou art, and unto dust shalt thou return'. And so shall we. This came first.

'The second man the Lord out of heaven.' He came down from heaven: 'I came down from heaven', John 6:38. 'And no man hath ascended up to heaven, but he that came down from heaven', John 3:13.

'Ye are from beneath; I am from above: ye are of this world; I am not of this world', John 8:23.

He ascended up to heaven: 'So then after the Lord had spoken unto them, he was received up into heaven', Mark 16:19.

'He was parted from them, and carried up into heaven', Luke 24:51. 'I ascend unto my Father, and your Father; and to my God, and your God', John 20:17.

He is in heaven, and is the heavenly man: the second man. 'The second man the Lord out of heaven', I Corinthians 15:47.

'And sat on the right hand of God', Mark 16:19.

'What and if ye shall see the Son of man ascend up where he was before?', John 6:62.

'Sat down on the right hand of the Majesty on high', Hebrews 1:3.

'The LORD said unto my Lord, Sit thou on my right hand, until I make thy foes thy footstool', Acts 2:34,35.

This is the heavenly man, a life-giving spirit, who is the firstfruits of them that slept. And as is the firstfruits, so will be the harvest.

'As is the earthy, such are they also that are earthy: and as is the heavenly, such are they also that are heavenly', I Corinthians 15:48.

But the translators repeat the same grievous and wholly unnecessary error, as will appear by comparison with the following interlinear literal translation: 'Such as he made of dust'–the Greek is *choikos*, not *gēs*; compare verse 47–'such also those made of dust; and such as the heavenly [one], such also the heavenly [ones].'

Where the seed springing from the Head and progenitor, bears the nature and image of him from whom their descent is counted, either the first, made of dust; or the second, come out of heaven.

'And as we have borne the image of the earthy, we shall also bear the image of the heavenly', I Corinthians 15:49.

'The Englishman's Greek-English New Testament', Bagster, 1877, reads: 'And according as we bore the image of the [one] made of dust, we shall bear also the image of the heavenly [one]', I Corinthians 15:49.

'As *we* bore'? '*We* shall bear also'? But who is *we*? It is those who first bore the image of the one made of dust. This is the image of the man who transgressed, the first man Adam, the man who brought in the Fall, the man of sin and death, formed from the earth, made of dust, cursed to return to dust. '*We*' bore that image.

We were born in and of that image, shapen in iniquity, conceived in sin: that was our nativity and our genealogy. We were sons of disobedience: that is, disobedience begat us, and disobedient we were.

There was no difference between us and others: *any* others.

We were the children of wrath, even as others: then, if so, wrath hung over the children of men; it overshadowed their conception; they were the children of it; the wrath of God in the curse preceded, anticipated, and accompanied their generation: 'children of wrath, even as others.'

It was by one man's disobedience, upon which came the curse, wrath, and judgment; by one man's disobedience we were made sinners: the whole generation, the entire seed, of that man of disobedience, appeared in the image of their progenitor, and, in him, passed under the judgment justly brought upon that man and his issue.

Having borne the image of the one made of dust, dust we were, dust we are, and unto dust shall we return. Namely, we shall return to dust by way of death and the grave; by way of corruption; of dishonour; of weakness; and of the flesh; of that decay and dissolution which is the inevitable end of all who bore the image of the one formed from the earth, made of dust, the first man Adam.

And *we* shall bear *also*? When all alike bore the image of the one made of dust? Then who are '*we*'? We are those of whom it is written, 'according as we bore the image of the [one] made of dust, *we* shall also bear the image of the heavenly [one]'.

Who are these? Not *all* who bore – or bear – the image of the one made of dust, but a people chosen out to be of the heavenly man, the second man, the last Adam.

If so, those brought under the power of the potter: 'Hath not the potter power over the clay, of the same lump to make one vessel unto honour, and another unto dishonour?

'What if God, willing to show his wrath, and to make his power known, endured with much longsuffering the vessels of wrath fitted to destruction: and that he might make known the riches of his glory on the vessels of mercy, which he hath afore prepared unto glory, even us, whom he hath called, not of the Jews only, but also of the Gentiles?', Romans 9:21-24.

Here is the 'we' of I Corinthians 15:49.

'For he saith to Moses, I will have mercy on whom I will have mercy, and I will have compassion on whom I will have compassion. So then it is not of him that willeth, nor of him that runneth, but of God that showeth mercy', Romans 9:15,16.

And again: 'Therefore hath he mercy on whom he will have mercy, and whom he will he hardeneth', Romans 9:18.

And who are these, the 'we', who, having first borne the image of the one made of dust, thereafter, called by grace, shall also bear the image of the heavenly one?

These are those spoken of in a certain place, saying, 'Blessed be the God and Father of our Lord Jesus Christ, who hath blessed us with all spiritual blessings in heavenly places in Christ: according as he hath chosen us in him before the foundation of the world, that we should be holy and without blame before him in love: having predestinated us unto the place of sonship by Jesus Christ to himself, according to the good pleasure of his will, to the praise of the glory of his grace, wherein he hath made us accepted in the beloved', Ephesians 1:3-6.

It is these, and none other, who 'shall bear the image of the heavenly one'.

Jesus spake of them, known of the Father before ever the heavens or the earth were formed, even from everlasting; given to the Son in the will, counsel, and purpose of God, so that they were seen in him before the world was created or Adam was fashioned from the dust of the ground.

'I have manifested thy name'–the name of Father–'unto the men which thou gavest me out of the world: thine they were, and thou gavest them me; and they have kept thy word', John 17:6.

'I pray for them: I pray not for the world, but for them which thou hast given me; for they are thine. And all mine are thine, and thine are mine; and I am glorified in them', John 17:9,10.

All these are of the heavenly one, hence he says, 'They are not of the world'–no, not in the will, counsel, and purpose of God; and now, called by grace, not in the man of dust either– 'even as I am not of the world', John 17:16.

'For whom he did foreknow, he also did predestinate to be conformed to the image of his Son, that he might be the firstborn among many brethren. Moreover whom he did predestinate, them he also called: and whom he called, them he also justified: and whom he justified, them he also glorified', Romans 8:29,30.

This is the 'we', and thus shall 'we' bear the image of the heavenly one.

These are the Father's; they are also the Son's: for all those who are the Father's are the Son's; and all those who are the Son's are the Father's.

Hence of them he saith, 'My Father, which gave them me, is greater than all; and no man is able to pluck them out of my Father's hand', John 10:29.

'All that the Father giveth me shall come to me', saith Jesus, 'and him that cometh to me I will in no wise cast out', John 6:37.

No, for 'I came down from heaven, not to do mine own will, but the will of him that sent me', John 6:38.

What will is this? 'This is the Father's will which hath sent me'– from heaven–'that of all which he hath given me I should lose nothing, but should raise it up again at the last day', John 6:39.

This 'raising up again' will appear in the image of the heavenly one, namely, of him that came down from heaven to do his Father's will.

As to those that come to him, this coming is not of blood, nor of the will of the flesh, nor of the will of man–how could it be? man is of the earth, made of dust–but it is out of heaven from God and the Father that these come to the Son.

Hence it shall and must follow, 'they shall be all taught of God. Every man therefore that hath heard, and hath learned of the Father'–saith the Son–'cometh unto me', John 6:45.

And to what end, but that every one of them shall 'bear the image of the heavenly one', being raised up at the last day.

'Now this I say, brethren, that flesh and blood cannot inherit the kingdom of God; neither doth corruption inherit incorruption', I Corinthians 15:50.

No. It does not, and it cannot. But yet we *are* in a body of flesh and blood, subject to corruption: what of this?

What of it? this has already been shown: *it must die first, then it shall rise to inherit.*

For, 'it is sown in corruption; it is raised in incorruption: it is sown in dishonour; it is raised in glory: it is sown in weakness;

119

it is raised in power: it is sown a natural body; it is raised a spiritual body', I Corinthians 15:42,43.

Then that flesh and blood, called 'this vile body', though it cannot inherit the kingdom of God, nevertheless *can* still *be sown*. And that is precisely what takes place: 'it *is* sown.' It can still *die*. And that is exactly what is written: '*it* is sown' in death.

Likewise, what happens to the body in the grave precludes the inheritance of the kingdom of God by its very state: 'neither doth corruption inherit incorruption.'

But though the grave claim the dead body, though corruption rot the corpse, *it is not that that is raised*.

Not that? No; what is *changed* is raised. And so it is written, 'It is sown in corruption; *it is raised in incorruption*.'

Moreover it is certain beyond all doubt that what is raised in incorruption; in glory; in power; and as a spiritual body, cannot fail to inherit the kingdom of God.

How shall this be? Through him who loved us, and gave himself for us: through Christ the firstfruits, 'who shall *change* our vile body, that it may be fashioned like unto his glorious body, according to the working whereby he is able even to subdue all things unto himself', Philippians 3:21.

Thus through Jesus Christ our Lord, the last Adam, a quickening spirit; through the second man, the Lord from heaven: though flesh and blood cannot, *we* can, and we *shall* inherit the kingdom of God; and though corruption cannot, *incorruption* can, and incorruption *shall* inherit the kingdom of God, to the praise of the glory of his grace, world without end. Amen.

The apostle had shown the folly of questioning the resurrection of the dead—and of asking presumptuous questions about it—first from the evidence manifest in creation, I Corinthians 15:35-41.

Next he proceeded to demonstrate the same thing by revelation, I Corinthians 15:42-50.

Finally he crowns this overwhelming body of inspired truth with the opening of a mystery, followed by a closing word of comfortable admonition, I Corinthians 15:51-58.

'Behold, I show you a mystery; We shall not all sleep, but we shall all be changed, in a moment, in the twinkling of an eye, at the last trump: for the trumpet shall sound, and the dead shall be raised incorruptible, and we shall be changed', I Corinthians 15:51,52.

Paul alerts the reader to what he is about to say: 'Behold'; directing the focus of their attention, and sharpening the concentration of their minds by this peremptory and anticipatory watchword.

To what? To the fact that he is about to unfold a mystery, so as to show them things hitherto veiled from their sight and comprehension: 'Behold!' here is a mystery, and he is about to show them what is in the will, mind, counsel, and purpose of God concerning things to come.

It cannot be overstressed that mysteries can never be understood: they can be shown, in the sense that the Seer can describe the vision uniquely unveiled to him. That is, he can make known what he has seen, whether by speech or in writing, to those to whom he is sent.

Nevertheless, despite any such speech or writing, God reserves his divine prerogative, because for all the description, *it requires the Spirit to make the thing described an interior reality to the reader and hearer.*

Furthermore, regarding the fact that the apostle is to show them a mystery, here is no appeal whatsoever to the intellect, to human reason, or to anything that man is capable of understanding mentally: it is solely an appeal to *faith.*

121

Mysteries, revealed or shown to the apostolic administration, or to the prophetic ministry in consequence, are *believed*. Not understood. Faith acts upon them. But understanding founders upon them.

This mystery – afore seen in vision and revelation by the apostle – which now is to be shown to the *ecclesia* at Corinth, concerns *what happens to the bodies of the quick and the dead; the living and the buried; of all who ever were, are, or shall be in Christ, when the last trumpet shall sound.*

This unfolds in two parts: What happens to the quick, or living bodies; and what happens to the dead, or buried bodies, respectively.

I Corinthians 15:51 tells you *that* we shall all be changed, whether it be all the dead, or all the living. In a word, *all* in Christ shall be changed, from the beginning of the world to the end of it.

But, next, I Corinthians 15:52 tells you *when* we shall all be changed, and how quickly, no matter that it be the dead out of every generation to the ends of the earth and from the depths of the sea, or whether it be the faithful remnant of the saints still living upon the earth in the instant that the great and last trumpet awakens the dead.

Notwithstanding, in each case, either *that* we shall all be changed; or *when* we shall all be changed, *the change referred to in the mystery is that of the body.*

First consider *that* we shall all be changed. It must be so, since, I Corinthians 15:50, 'flesh and blood cannot inherit the kingdom of God; neither doth corruption inherit incorruption'. Then it follows, because we *do* inherit the kingdom of God, and we *shall* inherit incorruption, that '*we shall* all be changed'.

To be precise, our *bodies*, of flesh and blood, shall be changed; and *our corruption*, mouldering in the grave, shall be changed. And in this change, there is a difference between the quick and the dead.

Why? Because 'we shall not all sleep', I Corinthians 15:51.

That is, our *bodies* shall not all sleep. Some shall *never die*: they shall be changed, as was Christ in the transfiguration, *whilst still alive in this present* – but dissolving – *world*.

No, we shall not all sleep, some shall be alive at his coming; nevertheless, we *shall* all be changed.

When? Ponder well *when* we shall all be changed, and how *quickly*, whether it be the dead, or the living:

'In a moment, in the twinkling of an eye, at the last trump: for the trumpet shall sound, and the dead shall be raised incorruptible' – *this* is first; fast as the twinkling eye blinks to a close – 'and *we* shall be changed' – *that* is next; swift as the twinkling eye flashes open. I Corinthians 15:52.

Neither are the 'sleeping' dead bodies of all that ever died in the faith, nor the living bodies of the believing remnant alive in the dying moments of time, *all* that shall be 'changed': Greek ἀλλαγησόμεθα, *from* ἀλλάσσω, *allassō, to make other; alter*.

For not only they, but at the last trump the heavens and the earth also shall be subject to the same 'change':

'And, Thou, Lord, in the beginning hast laid the foundation of the earth; and the heavens are the works of thine hands: they shall perish; but thou remainest; and they all shall wax old as doth a garment; and as a vesture shalt thou fold them up, *and they shall be changed*', Hebrews 1:10-12.

Where 'shall be changed' answers to the Greek ἀλλαγήσονται – apart from the slight difference in grammar at the ending, exactly the same word as in I Corinthians 15:51 and 52 – *from* ἀλλάσσω, *allassō, to make other; alter.*

As to *how* so stupendous a change shall take place in the very heavens and earth, and *how* so astounding a mystery as that of the resurrection of the dead in bodies of glory, and, at the blink of an eye, the transformation and transfiguration of the bodies of the living saints shall take place: why, it is by the word of the Lord.

'Who shall *change*' – μετασχηματίσει *from* μετασχηματίζω, *metaschēmatizō, transform; to make of another form* – 'our vile body, that it may be fashioned like unto his glorious body, according to the working whereby *he is able even to subdue all things unto himself*', Philippians 3:21.

'But of that day and hour knoweth no man, no, not the angels of heaven, but my Father only', Matthew 24:36. 'For when they shall say, Peace and safety; then sudden destruction cometh upon them, as travail upon a woman with child; and they shall not escape', I Thessalonians 5:3. 'And what I say unto you I say unto all, Watch', Mark 13:37.

'Watch therefore, for ye know neither the day nor the hour wherein the Son of man cometh', Matthew 25:13.

'But the day of the Lord will come as a thief in the night; in the which the heavens shall pass away with a great noise, and the elements shall melt with fervent heat, the earth also and the works that are therein shall be burned up.

'Seeing then that all these things shall be dissolved, what manner of persons ought ye to be in all holy conversation and godliness, looking for and hasting unto the coming of the day of God, wherein the heavens being on fire shall be dissolved, and the elements shall melt with fervent heat?

'Nevertheless we, according to his promise, look for new heavens and a new earth, wherein dwelleth righteousness', II Peter 3:10-13.

'For yourselves know perfectly that the day of the Lord so cometh as a thief in the night', I Thessalonians 5:2.

In that day, the trumpet shall be blown, even the last trump, as it is written, 'He shall send his angels with a great sound of a trumpet, and they shall'—mark, *they* shall: that is, to bear up the *bodies* of the risen saints—'gather together his elect from the four winds, from one end of heaven to the other', Matthew 24:31.

It is not that—in a figure—trumpets had not sounded before—six times, metaphorically, they had sounded before.

'And I saw the seven angels which stood before God; and to them were given seven trumpets.' 'And the seven angels which had the seven trumpets prepared themselves to sound', Revelation 8:2,6.

And they did sound. In an allegory the first four angels sounded, but the world heard nothing, and saw nothing, neither did the inhabitants of the earth understand anything.

Thereafter, in the figure, the severity increases:

'And I beheld, and heard an angel flying through the midst of heaven, saying with a loud voice, Woe, woe, woe, to the inhabiters of the earth by reason of the other voices of the trumpet of the three angels, which are yet to sound!', Revelation 8:13.

And, in the vivid imagery of the Book of the Revelation, 'The fifth angel sounded', Revelation 9:1; 'And the sixth angel sounded', Revelation 9:13.

Then, one remained: the last, seventh angel. One trumpet was yet to sound, that is, the last trump.

And sound it shall, not only in prophecy in the Revelation; but in reality, at the last day: 'And the seventh angel sounded', Revelation 11:15. To apprehend the sound thereof, read my book 'The Revelation of Jesus Christ', which I neither received of man, neither was I taught it, but by the revelation of Jesus Christ, Galatians 1:12.

Thenceforth, at the sounding of this seventh, last, trump, that also is brought to pass which is written: 'We shall not all sleep, but we shall all be changed, in a moment, in the twinkling of an eye, at the last trump: for the trumpet shall sound, and the dead' – which are in Christ – 'shall be raised incorruptible, and we shall be changed', I Corinthians 15:51,52.

This is that by which the apostle Paul consoles those whose brethren or sisters had died, for, in his comfortable words to them, he calls their dying 'falling asleep', saying:

'But I would not have you to be ignorant, brethren, concerning them which are asleep, that ye sorrow not, even as others which have no hope. For if we believe that Jesus died and rose again, even so them also which sleep in Jesus will God bring with him.

'For this we say unto you by the word of the Lord, that we which are alive and remain unto the coming of the Lord' – for we shall not *all* sleep – 'shall not prevent' – that is, anticipate, or come before – 'them which are asleep.'

No: for the trumpet shall sound, and *the dead* shall be raised incorruptible. *Then*, in the twinkling of an eye, *we* – which are alive and remain – *shall be changed.*

'For the Lord himself shall descend from heaven with a shout.' Mark that: first, a shout. This is the last word. It is the omega. The ending. This is the hour that is to come in which all that are in the graves *shall hear his voice*. In a shout. *And shall come forth*; they that have done good, unto the resurrection of life.

'With the voice of the archangel.' This is the angels, sent forth of the archangel, to minister for them that are the heirs of salvation, carrying their changed, transformed, transfigured bodies to meet the Lord in his coming.

It is his 'sending forth his angels with a great sound of a trumpet, and they shall gather together his elect from the four winds, from one end of heaven to the other.'

'And with the trump of God.' This is the 'great sound of a trumpet.' It is the sounding of the seventh angel with the last trump.

'For the trumpet shall sound, and the dead shall be raised incorruptible, and we shall be changed.'

Oh, mark well how it shall be in that day, in that hour: 'the Lord himself' – note that emphasis: *himself* – 'shall *descend from heaven*' – then, *that* is where he has been, *all this time*, ever since the ascension: but no more – 'descend from heaven with a shout, with the voice of the archangel, and with the trump of God: *and the dead in Christ shall rise first.*'

The dead in Christ shall rise *first*. Not that *all* of us shall have slept, or shall sleep. Some shall not. But *all* shall be changed.

In a moment, in the twinkling of an eye, at the last trump: for the trumpet shall sound, and the dead shall be raised incorruptible, and *we* shall be changed.

We shall be changed?

Yes, in the twinkling of an eye, as the dead are raised, the living saints shall be changed also: 'Then we which are alive and remain shall be caught up together with them in the clouds, to meet the Lord in the air: and so shall we ever be with the Lord. Wherefore comfort one another with these words', I Thessalonians 4:13-18.

'For this corruptible must put on incorruption, and this mortal must put on immortality. So when this corruptible shall have put on incorruption, and this mortal shall have put on immortality, then shall be brought to pass the saying that is written, Death is swallowed up in victory', I Corinthians 15:53,54.

Observe, 'This corruptible *must* put on incorruption, and this mortal *must* put on immortality.'

But why *must* it? Because of the truth enunciated earlier, 'Now this I say, brethren, that flesh and blood *cannot* inherit the kingdom of God; *neither* doth corruption inherit incorruption', I Corinthians 15:50.

Now, if *we* are to inherit the kingdom of God, but flesh and blood *cannot* inherit the kingdom of God, it follows that such an inheritance must require that we put off flesh and blood.

How? By death and the grave. Then this mortal *body* must, of necessity, be put off, the soul meanwhile being with the Lord.

'Not for that we would be unclothed'–that is, our soul unclothed from our body–'*but clothed upon*'–with what was sown in mortality, but raised in immortality–'*that mortality might be swallowed up of life*', II Corinthians 5:4.

If so, this mortal body–whether in the resurrection of the dead, or the transformation of the living, at the last trump–*must*, in the resurrection, put on immortality *in the body*, so that we, ourselves, may inherit the kingdom of God.

Then shall be brought to pass the saying that is written, 'Come, ye blessed of my Father, inherit the kingdom prepared for you from the foundation of the world', Matthew 25:34.

For this to take place, flesh and blood, the natural body, *must* be put off; and the resurrection of the dead, the transformation, the spiritual body, *must* be put on. And so Paul says, 'this mortal *must* put on immortality.'

Likewise 'neither doth corruption' – this corruptible body inhabited in this life, and corrupting in the grave thereafter, *cannot* inherit the kingdom, *not in that state* – hence, 'neither doth corruption inherit incorruption', I Corinthians 15:50.

Wherefore it follows of necessity, 'this corruptible' – body – 'must put on incorruption' – in the body raised from the dead. For, 'it is sown in corruption; it is raised in incorruption', where the *it* refers to *the body*, whether sown or raised.

Then, 'incorruption' refers to the body of glory, raised from the dead. '*It* is sown in dishonour; *it* is raised in glory: *it* is sown in weakness; *it* is raised in power: *it* is sown a natural body; *it* is raised a spiritual body', I Corinthians 15:42-44.

Wherefore he saith, 'neither doth corruption inherit incorruption', I Corinthians 15:50; concluding, 'For this corruptible *must* put on incorruption', I Corinthians 15:53.

'So when this corruptible shall have put on incorruption, and this mortal shall have put on immortality' – When? When we shall all be changed: in a moment, in the twinkling of an eye, at the last trump:

'For the trumpet shall sound, and the dead shall be raised incorruptible, and we shall be changed' – 'then shall be brought to pass the saying that is written, Death is swallowed up in victory', I Corinthians 15:54.

Death can no more be seen. It is swallowed up. It is as if death had never been: victory has swallowed up death and its effects wholly and utterly, so as to abolish it entirely. Who did this? Who wrought this victory? When and how was the last enemy annihilated to the uttermost?

It was determined of God when he sent his Son:

'Who hath saved us, and called us with an holy calling, not according to our works, but according to his own purpose and grace, which was given us in Christ Jesus before the world began, but is now made manifest by the appearing of our Saviour Jesus Christ,

'Who *hath'* – *hath; hath; past tense* – *hath* '*abolished death*' – swallowing it up in victory – '*and hath brought life and immortality to light through the evangel*', II Timothy 1:9,10.

Wherefore he saith, 'I am the resurrection, and the life: he that believeth in me, though he were dead, yet shall he live: and whosoever liveth and believeth in me shall never die', John 11:25,26. 'Christ the firstfruits; afterward they that are Christ's at his coming', I Corinthians 15:23.

And if so, and it is so, we may say, and that truly, 'O death, where is thy sting? O *hadēs*' – it is not *grave*: this is another blunder, and a shocking one, on the part of the translators – 'O *hadēs*, where is thy victory?', I Corinthians 15:55.

What more apt comment upon these words can there be, than that made by the apostle on another occasion, when triumphing in the victory won by Christ on behalf of all his people:

'What shall we then say to these things? If God be for us, who can be against us? He that spared not his own Son, but delivered him up for us all, how shall he not with him also freely give us all things? Who shall lay anything to the charge of God's elect? It is God that justifieth. Who is he that condemneth?

'It is Christ that died, yea rather, that is risen again, who is even at the right hand of God, who also maketh intercession for us.

'Who shall separate us from the love of Christ? shall tribulation, or distress, or persecution, or famine, or nakedness, or peril, or sword? As it is written, For thy sake we are killed all the day long; we are accounted as sheep for the slaughter.

'Nay, in all these things we are more than conquerors through him that loved us.

'For I am persuaded, that neither death, nor life, nor angels, nor principalities, nor powers, nor things present, nor things to come, nor height, nor depth, nor any other creature, shall be able to separate us from the love of God, which is in Christ Jesus our Lord', Romans 8:31-39.

As to death, 'he hath abolished death, and hath brought life and immortality to light through the evangel.' As to *hadēs*, 'What is it but that he also descended first into the lower parts of the earth?'

And then? Then, victorious over death and *hadēs*, he ascended up far above all heavens, *with every one of his elect seen in himself*. 'Wherefore he saith, When he ascended up on high, he led captivity captive, and gave gifts unto men', Ephesians 4:8.

'And without controversy great is the mystery of godliness: God was manifest in the flesh, justified in the Spirit, seen of angels, preached unto the Gentiles, believed on in the world, received up into glory', I Timothy 3:16.

Christ's victory over *hadēs* on behalf of all his people from the beginning of the world to the end of it has been opened at length in these pages under the heading 'The Body of Christ and the Gifts', I Corinthians 12:14-13:13, also published separately as a paperback.

Besides this, the tract 'The Mystery of Godliness' expounds the triumphant victory proclaimed in I Timothy 3:16, so that it is superfluous to reiterate the same wonderful truths in this place.

Suffice it to repeat with Paul his praise to the mighty Conqueror from the verses in context: 'Death is swallowed up in victory. O death, where is thy sting? O *hadēs*, where is thy victory?'

'The sting of death is sin; and the strength'—it is δύναμις, *dunamis*, power—'the *power* of sin is the law', I Corinthians 15:56. Now, what does *that* mean?

One thing is certain: no legalists either will or can explain the meaning of these words, for their content lies altogether beyond their experience.

But first, 'The sting of death is sin.' But since sin brings forth death—'for the wages of sin *is* death'—it follows that sin precedes death.

If so, one might expect this place to read, 'The sting of *sin* is death.'

But one would be wrong, for it does not so speak. Then here is yet another instance of the necessity of being led by the Spirit, so that scripture speaks for itself, as opposed to men speaking for scripture.

Then how is it that 'The sting of *death* is sin'? It is certain that the sting is in the tail, Revelation 9:10, and hence it is *after* death, by which the deceased have been stung, that the discovery is made as to the cause of the sting.

Sin, yes; but not *before* death, otherwise it could not be said, 'The sting *of death* is sin.'

Then, *after* death the sting is plunged into the terrified soul awakened to its unending and ever-conscious existence beyond the grave and for eternity.

In this life the vast majority refused to face two overwhelming criteria, towering above all others. The first is sin. The second, death.

But in the life to come, from the very moment of death, immediately the soul is brought face to face with these burning issues: first, that *their sin*, which they had ignored, *caused their death*.

And next, just a split second the other side of death, the sting strikes: *one must, but one cannot, pay the price of sin; neither can one find an atonement for it: it is too late.*

'And as it is appointed unto men once to die'–*then* comes the sting–'*but after this* the judgment', Hebrews 9:27. After this? After what? After death.

Then what? Then the judgment.

Judgment of what? Of all the vast accumulation of unpaid, unatoned sins against the law of God, and against the righteousness of God.

Then, *after death* comes the sting: *the sins ignored throughout life, and even unto death, pierce the soul through and through with a thousand barbs, for now the consciousness of one's being is wide awake to the reality that the debt incurred can never, no, never, be paid by the undying soul, world without end.*

This is the judgment of God on sin, realized too late after death, being the sting of death. And it is both final and irrevocable.

But this is not so of those found in Christ, for the Redeemer drew the sting on behalf of all the elect. 'Who his own self bare our sins in his own body on the tree', I Peter 2:24. 'So Christ was once offered to bear the sins of many', Hebrews 9:28.

'For this is my blood of the new testament, which is shed for many for the remission of sins', Matthew 26:28. 'Christ died for our sins according to the scriptures', I Corinthians 15:3. Then, there is neither death, nor sting, for the children of God.

'And the strength of sin is the law', I Corinthians 15:56. This is that law which those whited sepulchres, the blind Pharisees who call themselves 'reformed', tell us is the Christian's rule of life.

Well, Paul calls it the sentence of death; the rule of condemnation; a killing letter; a dreadful yoke; and assures us that far from directing us to righteousness and life it curses us, sin finding its strength and power in its very rule and commandment: 'the strength of sin *is the law*.'

But the strength of Christ is deliverance from the law.

'But now we are delivered from the law, that being dead wherein we were held', Romans 7:6. 'For I through the law am dead to the law, that I might live unto God', Galatians 2:19. 'For Christ is the end of the law for righteousness to every one that believeth', Romans 10:4.

'God sent forth his Son, made of a woman, made under the law, to redeem them that were under the law, that we might receive the place of sons', Galatians 4:4,5.

'For sin'–whose strength is *the law*–'shall not have dominion over you: for ye are not under the law, but under grace', Romans 6:14.

Then, for the elect, the power of sin, which is the law, is broken, because 'ye also are become *dead to the law* by the body of Christ', Romans 7:4; where, by his death, *and our death in him*, we are for ever beyond the reach of the law and the realm of legal jurisdiction.

If so, 'Thanks be to God, which giveth us the victory, through our Lord Jesus Christ.'

'Therefore, my beloved brethren, be ye steadfast, unmoveable, always abounding in the work of the Lord, forasmuch as ye know that your labour is not in vain in the Lord', I Corinthians 15:58.

JOHN METCALFE

Book Order Form

Please send to the address below:

	Price	Quantity
A Question for Pope John Paul II	£1.25	......
Of God or Man?	£1.45	......
Noah and the Flood	£1.90	......
Divine Footsteps	£0.95	......
The Red Heifer	£0.75	......
The Wells of Salvation	£2.35	......
The Book of Ruth (Hardback edition)	£4.95	......
Divine Meditations of William Huntington	£2.35	......
Present-Day Conversions of the New Testament Kind	£2.25	......
Saving Faith	£2.25	......
Deliverance from the Law	£1.90	......
The Beatitudes	£1.90	......
Pastoral Letters to the Far East	£2.00	......
Law and Grace Contrasted by William Huntington	£2.35	......
The Gifts and Baptism of the Spirit	£0.95	......
The Body of Christ and the Gifts	£0.95	......
The Coming Resurrection of the Dead	£0.95	......

Lectures from Church House, Westminster

		Price	Quantity
Colossians		£0.95	......
Philippians		£1.90	......
Matthew		£0.95	......
Philemon		£1.90	......
First Timothy		£2.00	......
Mark		£2.35	......
Creation		£2.00	......
The First Epistle of John (Hardback edition)		£9.25	......

Psalms, Hymns & Spiritual Songs (Hardback edition)

	Price	Quantity
The Psalms of the Old Testament	£2.50	......
Spiritual Songs from the Gospels	£2.50	......
The Hymns of the New Testament	£2.50	......

'Apostolic Foundation of the Christian Church' series

		Price	Quantity
Foundations Uncovered	Vol. I	£0.75	......
The Birth of Jesus Christ	Vol. II	£0.95	......
The Messiah (Hardback edition)	Vol. III	£7.75	......
The Son of God and Seed of David (Hardback edition)	Vol. IV	£6.95	......
Christ Crucified (Hardback edition)	Vol. V	£6.95	......
Justification by Faith (Hardback edition)	Vol. VI	£7.50	......
The Church: What is it? (Hardback edition)	Vol. VII	£7.75	......
The Revelation of Jesus Christ (Hardback edition)	Vol. VIII	£9.25	......

Name and address (in block capitals)

....

....

....

If money is sent with order please allow for postage. Please address to:- The John Metcalfe Publishing Trust, Church Road, Tylers Green, Penn, Bucks, HP10 8LN.

cut here

Tract Order Form

Please send to the address below:

		Price	Quantity
Evangelical Tracts			
The Two Prayers of Elijah		£0.10	......
Wounded for our Transgressions		£0.10	......
The Blood of Sprinkling		£0.10	......
The Grace of God that brings Salvation		£0.10	......
The Name of Jesus		£0.10	......
The Ministry of the New Testament		£0.10	......
The Death of the Righteous by A.M.S.		£0.10	......
Repentance		£0.10	......
Legal Deceivers Exposed		£0.10	......
Unconditional Salvation		£0.10	......
Religious Merchandise		£0.10	......
Comfort		£0.10	......
Peace		£0.10	......
Eternal Life		£0.10	......
The Handwriting of Ordinances		£0.10	......
'Lord, Lord!'		£0.10	......
Conversion		£0.10	......
'Tract for the Times' series			
The Gospel of God	No. 1	£0.25	......
The Strait Gate	No. 2	£0.25	......
Eternal Sonship and Taylor Brethren	No. 3	£0.25	......
Marks of the New Testament Church	No. 4	£0.25	......
The Charismatic Delusion	No. 5	£0.25	......
Premillennialism Exposed	No. 6	£0.25	......
Justification and Peace	No. 7	£0.25	......
Faith or Presumption?	No. 8	£0.25	......
The Elect Undeceived	No. 9	£0.25	......
Justifying Righteousness	No.10	£0.25	......
Righteousness Imputed	No.11	£0.25	......
The Great Deception	No.12	£0.25	......
A Famine in the Land	No.13	£0.25	......
Blood and Water	No.14	£0.25	......
Women Bishops?	No.15	£0.25	......
The Heavenly Vision	No.16	£0.25	......
The Mystery of Godliness	No.17	£0.25	......

Name and address (in block capitals)

....

....

....

cut here

If money is sent with order please allow for postage. Please address to:- The John Metcalfe Publishing Trust, Church Road, Tylers Green, Penn, Bucks, HP10 8LN.

Tract Order Form

Please send to the address below:

		Price	Quantity

Ecclesia Tracts

		Price	Quantity
The Beginning of the Ecclesia	No. 1	£0.10	......
Churches and the Church (J.N.D.)	No. 2	£0.10	......
The Ministers of Christ	No. 3	£0.10	......
The Inward Witness (G.F.)	No. 4	£0.10	......
The Notion of a Clergyman (J.N.D.)	No. 5	£0.10	......
The Servant of the Lord (W.H.)	No. 6	£0.10	......
One Spirit (W.K.)	No. 7	£0.10	......
The Funeral of Arminianism (W.H.)	No. 8	£0.10	......
One Body (W.K.)	No. 9	£0.10	......
False Churches and True	No.10	£0.10	......
Separation from Evil (J.N.D.)	No.11	£0.10	......
The Remnant (J.B.S.)	No.12	£0.10	......
The Arminian Skeleton (W.H.)	No.13	£0.10	......

Foundation Tracts

		Price	Quantity
Female Priests?	No. 1	£0.25	......
The Bondage of the Will (Martin Luther)	No. 2	£0.25	......
Of the Popish Mass (John Calvin)	No. 3	£0.25	......
The Adversary	No. 4	£0.25	......
The Advance of Popery (J.C. Philpot)	No. 5	£0.25	......
Enemies in the Land	No. 6	£0.25	......
An Admonition Concerning Relics (John Calvin)	No. 7	£0.25	......
John Metcalfe's Testimony Against Falsity in Worship	No. 8	£0.25	......
Brethrenism Exposed	No. 9	£0.25	......
John Metcalfe's Testimony Against The Social Gospel	No.10	£0.25	......

Name and address (in block capitals)

....

....

....

If money is sent with order please allow for postage. Please address to:- The John Metcalfe Publishing Trust, Church Road, Tylers Green, Penn, Bucks, HP10 8LN.

cut here

MINISTRY BY JOHN METCALFE

TAPE MINISTRY BY JOHN METCALFE
FROM THE U.K. AND THE FAR EAST
IS AVAILABLE

In order to obtain this free recorded ministry, please send your blank cassette (C.90) and the cost of the return postage, including your name and address in block capitals, to the John Metcalfe Publishing Trust, Church Road, Tylers Green, Penn, Bucks, HP10 8LN. Tapelists are available on request.

Owing to the increased demand for the tape ministry, we are unable to supply more than two tapes per order, except in the case of meetings for the hearing of tapes, where a special arrangement can be made.